WHAT'S

LOVE

GOT TO DO WITH

IT?

*To my uncle Johnny
and my aunt Irene
and my cousin Antoinette
~~+ Dave~~
        Phil.*

Philip J. Zeiter

WHAT'S
LOVE
GOT TO DO WITH
IT?

DISCOVERING TRUTH

DESIRING PEACE

DEVELOPING HAPPINESS

Fuel for the Journey of Life

Cover photograph:
"Sharing is Caring"
by Alicia K. Zeiter with
Ty-Ty and Zachy Zeiter
British Columbia, Canada

Cover design: Caroline Photography, Inc., Stockton, California

Second Printing: May, 2002

ISBN 0-9721446-0-9

© 2001 Mission of Peace
19626 Bear Hollow Road
Grass Valley, California 95949

by

an Educational Grant from the

Henry & Carol Zeiter Foundation
Lodi, California

Scripture quotations are taken from the *New International Version*
© 1973, 1978, 1984 Zondervan Publishing House, Grand Rapids, Michigan.

CONTENTS

DESIRING PEACE
DIVINE MOTIVATIONS

DEVELOPING HAPPINESS

DEDICATION

For those who have grown to realize
the everlasting quality of eternal life in
contrast to the temporal nature of this world —

May these meditations bring you closer to
the Divine Spirit who is our All.

For those who are struggling in this world alone —

May these meditations impress upon you
the existence of God, the reality of His truth,
and the happiness of His love.

PREFACE

Love leads to God and God leads to peace,
thus love leads to peace.

AND

The more peaceful we are, the happier we become.

"Peace I leave with you. My peace I give you."
(John 14:27)

*"As the Father has loved Me, so I have loved you.
Now remain in My love. . . .
I have told you this so that My joy may be in you
and that your joy may be complete."*
(John 15:9–11)

FOREWORD

All of the following information is based on the word of God as written in the Holy Bible. This author does not expect the reader to rely on his limited understanding and thereby substantiates each expressed truth with the teaching of Jesus Christ, the One Who is the Truth.

The New Testament of the Holy Bible documents the teachings of Jesus Christ. The books of Matthew, Mark, Luke, and John are eyewitness testimonies. Thus, the following quotations are the actual words of Christ.

"Therefore everyone who hears these words of mine and puts them into practice is like a wise man who built his house on the rock. The rain came down, the streams rose, and the winds blew and beat against that house; yet it did not fall because it had its foundation on the rock. But everyone who hears these words of mine and does not put them into practice is like a foolish man who built his house on sand. The rain came down, the streams rose, and the winds blew and beat against that house, and it fell with a great crash." (Matthew 7:24–27)

DISCOVERING TRUTH

1

WHAT IS GOD'S ROLE IN OUR JOY?

When I was born, the first thing I did was cry. I could have been thinking "Just put me back in 'cause it's cold and mean out here." Things didn't get much better those first few months. I was hungry, then tired, then hungry, then tired. Within a few years that cycle improved but then there were more babies. It seemed that I was always last. But as the years went by I found ways to get attention, sometimes by noise or trouble. But usually I acted politely and many times simple and pure. I didn't want to cause any problems; I only wanted love and affection.

I now see pictures of me in those years, always with a giant smile. People tell me that I was loving and happy. They say that I was a child of God. But what are they really saying? I hear about the innocence of youth. I hear people say that we are closest to God when we are little and without worries. They talk about the young as being God's loving and happy creatures. But what does love have to do with happiness? And what is God's role in our joy?

GOD GIVES US JOY

God exists in a state of perfect love, peace and happiness. He promises eternal life to everyone who desires Him. When we start learning about God, we naturally begin to love Him because He is so good and so beautiful. The more we know about God, the more we actually love Him, and the more we love God, the more we desire Him. When we desire God, life becomes a spiritual journey destined for union with Him, sharing in His happiness now and forever. God wants us to seek Him now and begin loving Him right here on earth, thus immediately enjoying His abundant peace. God offers His love to us now so that through it we may receive the true happiness it contains while we are in this world. He desires to establish loving relationships so that by following His commands we may grow in His love. **God invites us to share in His happiness starting right now and to remain in His joy forever.** *Blessed [happy] are they who follow the law of the Lord. Blessed [happy] are they who keep His statutes, and seek Him with all their heart.* (Psalm 119:1–2)

Forever is a long, long time. The human mind cannot fully comprehend eternity, but to begin to understand its infinite length we can make an earthly comparison. We can think of our lifetime as one small drop of water in comparison to the ocean of eternity. Envision one drop of water compared to the amount of water in a bucket, then a bathtub, then a swimming pool, then a large lake. How many drops of water are contained in an ocean? And even more drops comprise all of the oceans of the world. Yet heaven includes more lifetimes than all of those drops of water, filled with happiness and contentment. Eternity is an infinitely long time; it never ends. God wants us to enjoy it with Him in celebration. **God gives us this opportunity of life on earth as an exploration of love, to search for Him and find Him, that we may live with Him in peace now and forever.** *One thing I ask of the Lord, this is what I seek; that I may dwell in the house of the Lord all the days of my life, to gaze upon the beauty of the Lord and to seek Him in His temple.* (Psalm 27:4)

Some people who believe in God do not think about Him much here on earth. They just assume that when they die, God will correct their faults and they will progress directly to heaven. But that is a misunderstanding. We can only be in heaven when we have grown to a state of love which is compatible with God, enabling us to dwell with Him in harmony. It is necessary to learn about love while we are here on earth rather than after we die to this world. God wants the best for us and therefore offers the most expedient route to heaven. He wants us to develop ourselves here first so that when we pass on, we will already be prepared to join Him in heaven. God gives Himself to us now, guiding us along the path of love. He teaches us the laws of love (the Ten Commandments) so we can nurture love in ourselves by living according to His precepts. We thus adopt God's love in our hearts and receive His Spirit into our souls. By exerting effort to **know** God now we can **love** Him in this world and **serve** Him by loving others. By participating in God's love on earth, we properly mature in love here, complying with His desire while assisting Him in our salvation. We become more like God and more prepared to be with Him in heaven. *May Your unfailing love come to me, O Lord, Your salvation according to Your promise.* (Psalm 119:41)

Our life is a journey of love. It does not end when our body dies and neither does our quest for love. Our spirit remains alive and energized to start the next phase of our adventure. We pass from this world of time, space and matter to the spiritual domain. We become pure spirit while maintaining our identity, our intellect, our memory and our will.

This is all good news, but we need to realize that our personality can be a great help or a terrible hindrance to us at this juncture. Once purely spiritual, we receive a fuller knowledge of the goodness of God. **Upon this understanding of how beautiful love is in God, we will yearn to live in it with Him.** *I have seen You in the sanctuary and beheld Your power . . . Your love is better than life . . . earnestly I seek You; my soul thirsts for You, my body longs for You, in a dry and weary land where there is no water.* (Psalm 63:1–3) We may not be ready to join Him, however, and maybe not for a long time. Upon our death, the distance we have traveled in knowing, loving and serving God in this world will determine when we can rest with Him in paradise.

This opportunity for everlasting happiness and the necessity of working to attain it is the life into which we are all born. It is a beautiful and exciting journey requiring talent, enterprise and good will. God creates these qualities in us and allows us to use them in our community. Reaching heaven is not easy, however, because it requires love, and real love is not easy to acquire. To grow in love we must practice it, work at it and even struggle for it. To advance in love we must exercise charity, which demands humility and detachment. We must push ourselves to overcome our natural tendencies of pride and possessiveness.

To achieve the goal of eternal life we must conquer our bad habits, driving them out of our personality to make room for good habits and virtue. But let us take heart and have hope, because we have the power of God available to us. All that we need to do to receive His power is to desire it, and we do this by desiring Him. *I love You, O Lord, my strength. The Lord is my rock, my fortress, and my deliverer.* (Psalm 18:1–2)

We are not forced to desire God and His love. We have a choice. God created us with our own free will, our freedom to choose. We can accept our situation with love and goodness or we can deny it or be indifferent. Many people reject God before ever getting to know Him. These people have never experienced the deep and fulfilling happiness of God. But loving people are filled with joy, because happiness comes from love. And love comes from God. Therefore happiness comes from God. **Let us then strive for this joy-filled love by discovering its source in God.** *Let us love one another for love comes from God.* (1 John 4:7)

Can you imagine that there exists an all-loving, all-caring, benevolent and beautiful Being Who made us? That this Divine Spirit, in order to sustain us, gave us everything in the universe for our use and prosperity? That our one true God and Creator loves us so much that He wants us to be with Him forever in paradise? Well, it is true. And His happiness is not just an ordinary emotion. God's love generates a deep peace and a complete joy that fills our whole being. It creates an ecstasy we cannot contain. We are moved by the love of God and find Him so extraordinary that we want to share Him with everyone. **God's presence in people makes them excited to be alive, not lacking in any way, but completely fulfilled and content.** *I will praise You, O Lord, with all my heart; I will tell of Your wonders. I will be glad and rejoice in You.* (Psalm 9:1–2)

God's love inspires a desire for Him and an eagerness to join Him in heaven. So then, what is heaven like? It is a state of free-flowing happiness, resulting from the love of God. A state of such overwhelming peace that we cannot fully understand it until we enjoy the experience. *No eye has seen, no ear has heard, no mind has conceived what God has prepared for those who love Him.* (1 Corinthians 2:9) Can you imagine being one billion times happier than you have ever been? Can you give a blind man a pebble and have him understand a mountain by telling him it is one billion times larger than the pebble? But to consider the reality of heaven, just ponder being immersed in overwhelming peace while entirely filled with boundless joy, forever and ever and ever.

Do you want to be a part of heaven, a part of the All? Do you want to be a part of What Is? Or would you rather be lost in what is not? Do you want to exist? Or would you rather not exist? If you want to live, then you must be part of Existence — which is God. If you don't care much about life, upon learning God's truth you will become aware of His goodness and beauty. Then you will receive peace with an enthusiasm for life.

God is existence, He is life. If you want God, you choose life, but if you do not want Him, you choose death, whether willingly or not. *Before men are life and death, good and evil, whichever he chooses shall be given him.* (Sirach 15:15–20) God promises those who choose Him not only life, but life eternal. Just as our bodies need food, clothes and shelter, our souls have spiritual needs to survive. **When we choose God, we are fed with His love, clothed in His peace and sheltered within His happiness.**

The above questions and statements are made to evoke a response, a decision, a choice. Many people live most of their life without making this decision. In fact, most of us live in indecision or at least without full conviction. So then: do you believe in God? Many people, even when they answer "yes," give a slight shrug of the shoulders as if to say, "Yeah, pretty much, I think so." Let us challenge ourselves with more than just a casual response, and more than just an accidental hope. Let us incite ourselves to learn about God, that in discovering Him we can find His love and therein His peace and happiness. After all, God is the most important thing in life; actually, **God is life.** Therefore, the most important desire we can have is for a relationship with God. Then we can begin our spiritual journey to develop a relationship with Him. *You have made known to me the path of life; You will fill me with joy in Your presence, with eternal pleasures at Your right hand.* (Psalm 16:11)

2

WHO IS GOD, ANYWAY?

I always thought God was an obligation. Church was just some place that I was forced to go to. I never really wanted to be there but my parents told me it was good for me. They made me go and that made me bitter. It was just like that gushy yellow stuff they used to force down my throat at dinner. They said, "But it's good for you," only making it worse as they shoved a spoonful of squash in my mouth. It tasted good to my parents who wanted it, but to me it was like eating mud, one painful bite at a time. Just like going to church: peaceful and enriching to my parents, but anxious and painful to me.

My mind was not focused at church so I never really heard about God. I was busy thinking about all the fun I was missing. I didn't care to know God because it seemed He was blocking my fun. But then I saw people who were happy without depending on fun. They said they were happy because of God, not because of any worldly pleasure. But my life without God was boring and empty. How does God make people happy? Who is God, anyway?

GOD IS WHO IS

Any attempt to describe God would fall infinitely short of Who God is. Therefore what follows is an introduction to understanding God, not attempting to describe Him fully, but to provide a basic knowledge of Him — building blocks for a deeper relationship with Him. The best way to learn about God is through His revelation to us. In most cases, God reveals Himself to an individual only when that person asks. *"Ask and you shall receive; seek and you shall find; knock and the door will be opened to you."* (Matthew 7:7)

Right now, before reading any further, you can ask God to reveal Himself. If you do not yet know God within a personal relationship, this request is vital to your life. If you know about God but do not yet feel a deep, inner knowledge and resulting love for Him, then you too may gain by asking. If you currently know God intimately, and thereby love Him deeply, remember that as your knowledge of God grows, so does your love for Him.

God is existence, goodness, truth and beauty. From the Bible we know of Moses. He was instructed by God to deliver the Jews from Egypt, freeing them from years of slavery. Upon learning of his mission, Moses asked God, "Suppose I go to the Israelites and say to them, 'The God of your fathers has sent me to you,' and they ask me, 'What is his name?' Then what shall I tell them?" God gave Moses an answer that would serve all future generations. *God said to Moses, "I AM*

WHO I AM. This is what you are to say to the Israelites: I AM has sent me to you." (Exodus 3:14) God did not identify Himself as "I am this" or "I am that particular thing," as we could say about ourselves: "I am a human being," or "I am a man," or "I am a woman." Nor did God dictate to Moses an elaborate definition that would only confuse us. God wanted to give Moses an answer that we could understand, so to describe His All in human words He simply said, "I AM." **This means not only that God is everything, God is existence itself.**

Within His Entirety, God is goodness, truth, and beauty. Goodness is the state of being virtuous. God is all that is good and therefore maintains all virtue: kindness, generosity, understanding, forgiveness, compassion, gentleness, patience, serenity, tranquility and peace. God's goodness includes His infinite love which shines brightly in creation through His tremendous gifts. He starts giving to us by creating our very being. He then gives us the qualities of love to help us to become good like Him.

God, being the maker of all things is the Master of all things. *O Lord, our Lord, how majestic is Your name in all the earth!* (Psalm 8:9) Worldly rulers seldom give much of anything to their subjects. Even when they do give, it is in limited portions and in selfish ways, based on what they receive in return: image, political standing or votes. God, however, is the King of all kings and of all things, and in His goodness gives to us in bountiful portions without selfish reasons. God is entirely self-sufficient and needs nothing in return for His favors. He holds no ulterior motive. He gives us life and everything in it simply from His pure goodness. Even more significantly, He grants us the gift of His very Self. How lucky we are! How thankful we should be! The Supreme Being is so generous that He gives us Himself. God grants us His time whenever we want Him and His love whenever we need Him. He is always ready and willing to help us. God invites us to join Him and to share in His goodness. He gives us His love unceasingly. *The Lord has done great things for us, and we are filled with joy.* (Psalm 126:3)

God is the Truth — the Reality. God is the Intelligent Being, Who creates and maintains all life. He is the Oneness of all things and beings; the All of what we know. God is also everything we do not know, what we cannot see, and what is not of this world. With respect to beings, God is the whole and we are the parts. We often incorrectly refer to God as a part of our life. A more appropriate phrasing is that we are a part of His life. God is primary existence in which we take a role. We did not make our own life to share with God, rather He created us to share in His Life. We do not exist by our own power but through God's energy which sustains all life. He is allowing us to participate in His universe. *I lie down and sleep; I wake again, because the Lord sustains me.* (Psalm 3:5)

We have each been given our own identity but we are all dependent on God. We are all parts of the same Totality made in the image of God. *So God created man in His own image, in the image of God He created him; male and female He created them.* (Genesis 1:27) We are present in this world for a period of time. Upon completing this phase of living, if we have aspired to remain in God, we shall advance toward Him, ultimately progressing to union with Him. *The body is a unit, though it is made up of many parts; and though all parts are many, they form one body. So it is with Christ. For we were all baptized with one Spirit into one body.* (1 Corinthians 12:12)

Our need to be with God is demonstrated by our daily restlessness. We make continual plans for business, athletics, and recreation. We keep schedules that are filled for weeks and sometimes even months. As soon as one activity is canceled we start thinking about a possible replacement, and quickly make another commitment. Most of us find it difficult to relax even for a few minutes. We can verify this fact by sitting alone without any physical stimulation or disturbance. If we empty our minds of all worldly thoughts, most of us would feel uncomfortable or bored, usually within several minutes. Now let us imagine sitting there for one full day or even a week, let alone a month or a year. Most of us could not even make it past the first few hours without extreme agitation because we are not self-sufficient. We are naturally restless. We are fully dependent on God, Who is wholly sufficient without any needs. He is completely happy and content in Himself, never needing any change. We can thus find peace only through Him. **It is only in God that we enjoy true**

peace because He is Who makes us complete. *My soul finds rest in God alone; my salvation comes from Him.* (Psalms 62:1)

God is beauty — the quality of being pleasing. The term "pleasing" suggests two characteristics. First, that which is pleasurable; and second, that which is satisfying. God is then pleasure that is satisfying. The pleasure of God is permanent and thereby fulfilling. Completely satisfying pleasure giving everlasting fulfillment is perfect happiness. Therefore, God is perfect happiness. God's happiness is better than fun because His happiness is everlasting. The fun we have on earth is brief and usually gone soon after it comes. When is the last time you had fun? Where is it now? Gone! We cannot give much value to worldly fun because it is only temporary. Something that appears worthwhile can only be valuable if it lasts a long time. For what good is a new roof that leaks in the second rain? And who would buy a ring that was made out of straw? The happiness of God lasts forever, so it is something desirable, something of real value. *You will fill me with joy in Your presence, with eternal pleasures at Your right hand.* (Psalm 16:11)

God's beauty generates true happiness. When we include God in our activities we can truly enjoy the events, finding in them a true joy from God. However, when we exclude Him from our actions, we eliminate our lasting joy. For example, excessive drinking may be fun for a moment but will leave us with an awful hangover. Unlawful sexual intercourse may give temporary pleasure, but awkward feelings or guilt are usually the result. Regardless of the consequences of fun without God, one result is certain — afterward we want more fun. The more we have fun, the more we want fun, never to be satisfied. Worldly pleasure without love is insatiable and ultimately causes problems rather than joy. And life without love is frustrating because no matter how much fun we have, we are always left with a void. **Worldly fun begins with the promise of fulfillment, but it leaves us empty with an insatiable desire for more.** *I said to the Lord, "You are my Lord; apart from You I have no good thing."* (Psalm 16:2)

Conversely, happiness in God is totally fulfilling. God's happiness is exciting, enlivening and uplifting. It gives us contentment and it leaves us in peace, entirely complete. It does not leave us wanting to receive more but rather wanting to *give* more. God's happiness starts with the promise of fulfillment and delivers more than we ever knew, leaving us happy and full. In fact, it leaves us with such abundant joy that we are filled with enthusiasm. We then wish to share this peace with others rather than worry about receiving it ourselves.

This selflessness exists because peace comes from love and love does not diminish. Our actions of love create more love in us. When we grow in God's love we also grow in His peace because God's love produces peace within us. His peace then generates a continual joy. When God's love, peace and happiness exist within us, we experience His gift of fulfillment. **We become** enamored with His Goodness, energized by His Truth and enchanted in His Beauty. *The Lord is my shepherd, I shall not want. He makes me lie down in green pastures, He leads me beside still waters, He restores my soul.* (Psalm 23:1–3)

3

IS GOD A PERSON WE CAN KNOW?

After my early years, I saw that people who believe in God are people who are happy. But then I doubted the existence of God. I feared that He was just another fairy tale; another one of the grownups' stories made up to excite the children. I was worried that if I believed in God, I would soon be disappointed and sad. On several Christmas eves, I waited up all night with cookies on the table and a smile on my face. But Santa never showed up. My hope slowly melted away leaving me disappointed.

My big smile shrank and dimmed and my life became less without hope. Normally enjoyable activities became boring to me unless I was the center of attention. I didn't know what was wrong at the time but the problem eventually became clear. Without a strong belief in God there is nothing eternal to hope for. Most of my worldly hopes did not live up to my expectations so they often left me disappointed. But then I met people who were satisfied. It seemed like they actually knew God. But is God a person we can know? Is He really someone Who cares?

GOD IS THREE PERSONS IN ONE

The great Oneness of Life is an intelligent Being, Who wants us to know Him. He encompasses the height of reason and the purpose of all existence and action. In His divine wisdom, God manifests Himself as three Persons in One, the Holy Trinity: God the Father, God the Son, and God the Holy Spirit. Each Person co-exists with the others, fully knowing and sharing one anothers' will. To help us understand this concept of three in one, nature provides many examples. Every tree is composed of individual parts that exist together to form an organic whole. The roots, branches and leaves are all separate pieces, yet together form a tree. The roots gather nutrients, the branches provide structure and the leaves receive sunlight. Each part moves individually while acting together for the purpose of life.

Likewise, each person of the Holy Trinity maintains an individual function while acting together. God the Father is the Origin of the Trinity and the Creator of all things and beings. God the Son is the Word of the Trinity and the Savior of all human beings. God the Holy Spirit is the Love of the Trinity and the living presence in all human beings. Together as three persons in one, the Holy Trinity creates, maintains and dwells within all life. **God created us from the goodness of His love, maintains us by the truth of His love and fills us with the beauty of His love.**

This love of the Holy Trinity shines forth in the Divine Will: to establish an everlasting relationship with each one of us. *For God so loved the world that He gave His one and only Son, that whoever believes in Him shall not perish but have eternal life.* (John 3:16)

Even though we do not fully respond to His loving desire, God continues to love us unconditionally. God knows us and loves us whether or not we know Him. Because of His great love for us, God continues to extend the opportunity to everyone for a relationship with Him. When we don't participate in this relationship, God's fire of love and life fades in us, eventually diminishing to a tiny spark, awaiting a rekindling accomplished only through prayer. However, when we do make efforts to know and love God, the relationship is able to grow. We receive God more fully as our knowledge of Him grows. Then our love for Him grows and develops our love for others. We then experience an inner peace and a joy only known to those who are friends of God. He establishes a relationship with us through each person of the Holy Trinity. **The Father is our provider, the Son is our friend and the Holy Spirit is our instructor.**

God the Father provides for us first by giving us life. *God formed the man from the dust of the ground and breathed into his nostrils the breath of life, and the man became a living being.* (Genesis 2:7) He continues to sustain us in life by His constant awareness of us, and His desire for our existence. *Even the very hairs of your head are all numbered.* (Matthew 10:30)

The Father provides all the necessities for our physical survival; the food we eat, the clothes we wear and the roof under which we sleep. Each individual works to procure these things for himself, but they are first placed there by the Father for our use and consumption. The Father also gives us what we need to acquire these things.

God the Father gives us everything, including our soul — our spirit which lives forever. The Father provides us with spiritual food to help us grow in love. We desperately need these spiritual provisions because left to ourselves we cannot love. It is only from God the Father, the Source of all goodness and truth, that we can acquire love . . . *for love comes from God.* (1 John 4:7)

God the Son befriends us by sharing the Father's love. Everything that comes from the Father proceeds through the Son. All things and beings were created by the Father and made through the Son. *In the beginning was the Word, and the Word was with God, and the Word was God. He was with God in the beginning. Through Him all things were made; without Him nothing was made that has been made.* (John 1:1–3) God the Son is Jesus Christ. The One who came from heaven to earth upon Whose birth all time and history have been referenced. *The Word became flesh and made his dwelling among us.* (John 1:14)

Jesus Christ, the Son of God, is our own personal Friend and Savior. He came from the most peaceful and comfortable kingship, next to His Father in heaven, into the poorest of material surroundings on earth. The Son came into this world as our Friend to love us and to save us from death. He became our living example of love, guiding us by His words and actions. He paved for us the path of love which leads to the Father of all love in heaven. *I am the way and the truth and the life. No one comes to the Father except through Me.* (John 14:6) As our friend, He lived His entire earthly life never thinking of Himself. He acted only by the will of the Father for our salvation. His greatest desire is that we all come to know, love and serve the Father and thereby inherit eternal life with the Holy Trinity in heaven.

The Holy Spirit dwells within us. He shapes our morality by helping us recognize what is good and what is evil. We have all been created with a conscience, an awareness of right and wrong with an inclination to do what is right. This inclination is the manifestation of the Holy Spirit within us. He assists our understanding of right and wrong and He generates in us the desire to do that which is right.

When we have to make a choice between right and wrong, we tend to choose the easiest course of action. We also have a natural tendency to choose what we think will give us pleasure. Sometimes we choose an evil under the appearance of good. Because of our imperfections, it is impossible for us to always choose the highest and best good for ourselves. But the Holy Spirit helps us by teaching us how to act. He gives us the instructions and strength we need to make the right decisions. He is the interpreter of truth for us and the indwelling source of our wisdom. *We have not received the spirit of the world but the Spirit Who is from God, that we may understand what God has freely given us. This is what we speak, not in words taught us by human wisdom but in words taught by the Spirit, interpreting spiritual truths to spiritual men.* (1 Corinthians 2:12)

DESIRING PEACE
PERSONAL MOTIVATIONS

4

LIVING FOREVER

It didn't take me long to realize that nothing in this world is free. Even as early as grade school, I knew that "There's no such thing as a free lunch." Everything I saw in the world took a lot of pain to get. Everything seemed to cost too much. And when the trinket was finally acquired, it was soon lost or broken. Even with my young eyes, I saw many shattered dreams. And I heard the old people saying that dreams don't put food on the table, dreams don't put clothes on your back, and dreams don't put a roof over your head.

So why should I bother with paradise — after all, it's the dream of all dreams. But most people believe in life after death and most people say it is eternal. So does heaven really exist? What is it and where can we find it?

THE PRIZE OF HEAVEN

Heaven is the state of being eternally one with God. *"I pray . . . that all of them may be one, Father, just as You are in Me and I am in You. May they also be in us."* (John 17:20) Because God exists independent of location, heaven is not in any particular place but exists outside of space. Because God exists irrespective of measure, heaven exists outside of time. Space and time are creations of God that embody the physical world, but are not necessary in the spiritual realm of heaven. Human beings are created by God as both physical and spiritual, existing as both matter and spirit; that is, body and soul. Upon our bodily death in this world, our soul will not die but remain as living spirit, accountable for our actions in this world. Hopefully, we will have acted according to God's Word so that we may remain with Him forevermore in heaven. *"If you obey my commands, you will remain in My love, just I have obeyed my Father's commands and remain in His love."* (John 15:10)

God is eternal. He lives forever. Heaven is therefore eternal too. So as God invites us to join Him in heaven, He invites us to join Him forever. *For You granted Him authority over all people that He might give eternal life to all those You have given Him.* (John 17:2) God wants us to live with Him in perfect happiness forever. It is one thing to be offered eternal life and even greater to be promised an eternity of bliss. In heaven there is no trouble or sickness — there exists no disease, hunger or pain, loss or disappointment — no deficiency of any kind. In heaven there is only joy. **In heaven we shall be filled with pure love which generates peace and perfect joy.** To better understand this state, let us recall moments in our lives when we have experienced pure love. Think of yourself as a parent being away on a trip for a few days separated from your child. Upon your return, you greet her with a great embrace not wanting to let go. At that moment your mind is blank with no other care in the world. Nothing distracts your attention from your little child.

Think of when you were a young person with your first sweetheart, when everything seemed to separate you until you finally had a moment alone. You were able to embrace with a hug that you wanted to last forever. All current problems vanished leaving no care in the world. No thoughts appeared worthy — peace and joy filled your whole being.

Consider yourself newly-wed and on your honeymoon. The traveling is finally completed with no unfinished jobs, chores or stress — only you and your spouse remain. There in a low lit room, you snuggle up together next to a fire. You both realize that you're now married. With years of dreaming who it would be, and when and where it would happen; there you are, all of a sudden, gazing into each other's eyes. At that moment there is not a care in the world, not even a single thought. There are no distractions because you are captivated, entranced in love. You don't want to be anywhere else. You don't even want to move for fear the moment will slip away. An enlivening joy from deep within you emanates out toward your love. This mystical moment of peace: you wish it could last forever. You are fully content in love, and happy with an internal joy that captures your entire being. *"The kingdom of God is within you."* (Luke 17:21)

This is pure love as we find it in this world. It is God's love manifested within us in a minute form. What an embodiment of joy and comfort — a glorious taste of the happiness of heaven that God gives us here on earth! True love generates wonderful feelings that provide a hint of the happiness of heaven.

And heaven consists of more than a partial happiness. A slight disturbance can disrupt love in this world while divine love is ever-present. The love we experience in this world is one-dimensional, while the divine love of heaven is not constrained by space or time. Divine love sustains a stream of happiness in us which flows forever. *Whoever drinks the water I give him will never thirst. Indeed, the water I give him will become in him a spring of water welling up to eternal life.* (John 4:14)

Think of a time of deep love that you have experienced. Consider the incredible joy you discovered in that moment of peace. That state of joy and comfort exemplifies God's promise of life in heaven. We will enjoy pure love flowing in us and through us. We will rest, carefree, with no problems, worries, anxieties or distractions. **God's love in heaven generates abundant peace, maintaining us in perfect joy.**

In heaven we will rest in this state of pure happiness permanently. Moments of comfort on earth are often interrupted by unexpected events. We might be engaged in something we really enjoy when suddenly the telephone rings. The most trivial occurrence can easily upset a peaceful occasion. In heaven, however, nothing can change this gift of eternal love. There love abounds in everything and we are continuously immersed in love for all things and all beings.

This deep love for one another is never compromised by envy or jealousy. All love abides first in God and is dispensed to everyone through Him. God's love is thus maintained in perfect harmony for all who dwell in heaven. The happiness generated by God's love in heaven is perfect and always complete. *"I have told you this so that my joy may be in you and that your joy may be complete."* (John 15:11)

5

HAPPINESS IN HEAVEN

One of my strongest memories of school is my parents pressuring me for better grades. My teachers said that I didn't apply myself and that I could do much better. But all I wanted was to pass. I just wanted to get by. So I only did the minimum required. That approach seemed to prevail in other things too. When I was told to clear the table, I would often stop short by not putting the leftover food away. If I was to clean the dishes, the pots and pans would remain. I didn't care that I left work undone. It didn't bother me to cause someone else work. But I didn't know that someday I would have to give account for my lukewarm approach.

I remember missing the mark many times but my attitude was "oh, who cares." But some people say, "You only live once, so you better do your best while you can." I once flunked a class in school and it hurt, but isn't life different from school? I wonder now what my grade is for life and does it really matter? Is the afterlife based on our performance on earth? Is heaven the same for everyone?

DEGREES OF HAPPINESS IN HEAVEN

Everyone in heaven is filled with God's love, peace and joy. This bliss is maintained through each person's intimacy with the Father, as manifested through the Son, together with the Holy Spirit. Each person in heaven is established in an intimate relationship with the Holy Trinity from which is derived his share in God's Glory. *"I have given them the glory that You gave Me, that they may be one as We are one: I in them and You in Me. May they be brought to complete unity to let the world know that You sent me and have loved them even as you have loved me."* (John 17:22)

In heaven, the degree of intimacy with God varies from person to person. Thus each person will receive a different degree of happiness. While on earth, Jesus heard His closest disciples (the twelve apostles) argue about who among them would be the greatest. *Sitting down, Jesus called the twelve and said, "If anyone wants to be first, he must be the very last, and the servant of all."* (Mark 9:35) A while later, Jesus again spoke to the apostles and said, *"You know that those who are regarded as rulers of the gentiles lord it over them, and their high officials exercise authority over them. Not so with you. Instead, whoever wants to become great among you must be your servant, and whoever wants to be first must be slave of all. For even the Son of Man did not come to be served, but to serve, and to give His life as a ransom for many."* (Mark 10:42)

God is clear about the conditions necessary for eternal life. We must believe in Jesus and love one another. *And this is His command: to believe in the name of His Son, Jesus Christ, and to love one another as He commanded us.* (1 John 3:23) To teach us how to love each other, God gave us the Ten Commandments. He wants us to act in accordance with these laws of love because the extent of our response on earth determines our happiness in heaven. *"Anyone who breaks one of the least of these commandments and teaches others to do the same will be called least in the kingdom of heaven, but whoever practices and teaches these commands will be called great in the kingdom of heaven."* (Matthew 5:19)

Jesus summarized the Ten Commandments in one general rule: *"Do to others as you would have them do to you."* (Luke 6:31) By our actions here and now, we establish a degree of love in us. We exercise this love more or less, depending on the self-gratification we seek as opposed to the amount of attention we give others. The love we give in this world will form our lot in the next. *"Give and it will be given to you. A good measure, pressed down, shaken together and running over, will be poured into your lap. For the measure you use, it will be measured to you."* (Luke 6:38)

The variety of individual responses to God's love generates a variety of rewards available to us. *"In my Father's house are many rooms."* (John 14:2) In order to grow into greater love on earth, thus attaining more happiness in heaven, we need to progress in humility. **Humility is not only a condition for love but a prerequisite to eternal life.** *"Unless you change and become like* *little children, you will never enter the kingdom of heaven. Therefore, whoever humbles himself like this child is the greatest in the kingdom of heaven."* (Matthew 18:3–4) Those who know humility are those who know love. Consider the arrogant man who rarely listens to others. His conversations usually regard his own affairs, and the objects of his affection are his own activities. He does not normally assist the needy because it gets in the way of the valuable time he reserves for himself. His actions display little love to others and it is difficult for others to love him. But the humble man makes time for others and listens to their opinions. He prefers discussions of their ideas rather than his own. And he is willing to lend a helping hand. His attention is directed toward others so he is patient and kind. These actions demonstrate selfless love and promote affection in return. As others appreciate his humble demeanor they acknowledge him in high esteem. And God grants this polite man favors by helping him achieve his dreams. *"The greatest among you will be your servant. For whoever exalts himself will be humbled, and whoever humbles himself will be exalted."* (Matthew 23:11–12)

Let these words of God inspire us to live a life of love — a life of giving and helping others rather than a life of self-centered concerns. Our happiness in heaven will be proportionate to our actions here in this world. *The Lord has dealt with me according to my righteousness; according to the cleanliness of my hand He has rewarded me.* (Psalm 18:20) Each soul may be described as a container to be filled with God's love and its ensuing happiness, with each one made of a different size. Some will develop into great lakes of love while others will remain the size of a thimble. Each soul will be filled to the brim with happiness, yet some will contain a greater joy than others. Intimacy with God in heaven is developed by loving Him in this world. **We increase our reward of heavenly joy by increasing our love while here on earth.**

God gives us opportunities to grow in love through situations we encounter. When we act for the benefit of others instead of for ourselves, we make an act of love. Our love increases each time that we give, obtaining a deeper love for us to enjoy in heaven. Thus, our actions now have a direct impact on the level of joy that we will experience for all eternity. *God will give to each person according to what he has done.* (Romans 2:6)

Sometimes acts of love are difficult and sometimes they can be painful. But for the sake of heavenly love and to remain in ecstasy forever it is certainly worth the effort. To fully understand the importance of life, let us again consider the eternal qualities of heaven. Mount McKinley in Alaska is twenty thousand, three hundred and twenty feet high. If once each day an eagle lands on the peak, then pushes away in flight, its claws will scratch the granite surface and rub off a tiny portion. Each day an eagle returns and upon its departure brushes off another smidgen of rock. The time that it takes for the entire mountain to flatten is not even a moment in the realm of paradise. We are given control to shape our future. How we use our free will determines the way we spend everlasting life.

We therefore have an obligation to ourselves to love more in this world, that we may enjoy more happiness in the next. But how can we learn to love more on earth? It seems that the majority of our actions here are self-centered and self-seeking. We need to overcome our human tendency to act in selfish ways. *With man this is impossible, but not with God; all things are possible with God.* (Mark 10:27) We need to act generously and pray to God for the gift of love, for He is love. We need God in us so that we too can love. Then we can be happy. *"I have made You known to them, and will continue to make You known in order that the love You have for Me may be in them and that I Myself may be in them."* (John 17:26)

6

RECEIVING GIFTS FROM GOD

I went to a Catholic school from grades one through eight. Around the seventh and eighth grades there was teaching about the sacraments of God instituted by Christ for His Church. We were supposed to start preparing ourselves for the sacrament of Confirmation. There we would confirm our baptismal declaration for Christ, now that we could speak for ourselves. God lives within us and He comes to us in a special way at Baptism. We grow as Christians when the Holy Spirit comes to renew and strengthen us during Confirmation.

I thought I had grown enough already because I didn't prepare for the sacrament. But the adults were solemn and respectful, emphasizing the importance of this divine activity. One parent discussed his spiritual life. "Upon my Confirmation," he said, "I never felt lonely again. I developed my relationship with God starting then and will never lose Him again." What happens in us at Baptism and Confirmation? Does God really dwell in us?

THE SPIRIT WITHIN

God manifests Himself in us through Jesus, together with the Holy Spirit. *"The Holy Spirit, whom the Father will send in My name, will teach you all things and will remind you of everything I have said to you."* (John 14:26) The Holy Spirit comes into us at baptism and is deepened in us at Confirmation. *"I baptize you with water, but He [Jesus] will baptize you with the Holy Spirit."* (Mark 1:8) The Holy Spirit brings to us great gifts from God, the seedlings of virtue: faith, hope and charity. As our instructor, the Holy Spirit starts our training by giving us faith, which is belief in God; hope, which is trust in God; and charity, which is love in God. As we pray and practice these virtues, they grow and develop in us. *Don't you know that you yourselves are God's temple and that God's Spirit lives in you?* (1 Corinthians 3:16)

Our seedling of faith sprouts with a basic knowledge of God. When we learn the Truth of God, we become more inquisitive, enchanted by His goodness and beauty. We learn about His wonderful gifts. We begin to appreciate God, while coming more and more to believe in Him. This belief in God springs forth into faith, rooted in us with the Holy Spirit. Our faith in God naturally gives us hope as we trust in His promises. We trust in the "good news" of eternal life as given to us through Jesus. Our eternal happiness becomes the primary object of our hope. Hope is the desire for what is good, so we hope in the promises of God —

the promises of love. Our seedling of hope grows with our faith, grounded in the presence of the Holy Spirit. Our faith and hope in God cause us to love one another. We start by loving God through gratitude and the love He returns to us forms the charity we have for others. Due to our faith and hope in God, we love one another through Him. The flower of charity blooms from our faith and hope in God, flourishing in us with the Holy Spirit.

The goodness of God becomes alive in us through the gifts of the Holy Spirit. These gifts include kindness, generosity, understanding, forgiveness, compassion, gentleness, patience and tranquility, and by nature contain that which is good, while together define that which is love. *Love is patient, love is kind. It does not envy, it does not boast, it is not proud. It is not rude, it is not self-seeking, it is not easily angered, it keeps no record of wrongs. Love does not delight in evil but rejoices with the truth. It always protects, always trusts, always hopes, always perseveres.* (1 Corinthians 13:4–7)

Love is different than anything we encounter in the natural world because it is a supernatural grace from God. *"I am the light [love] of the world. Whoever follows Me will never walk in darkness [evil], but will have the light of life."* (John 8:12) *"You are from below; I am from above. You are from this world; I am not of this world."* (John 8:23) Jesus clearly indicates that love does not originate from this world, but is present only through Him as a gift from the Father. Common sense confirms this eternal truth because love is the only thing

on earth that does not diminish. Everything else decreases when used, but the more love that is given, the
more love there is. Virtues are not self-depleted, rather
they increase according to their use. The more kind
we are to others, the more kind we become. Thus,
kindness grows stronger within us the more we give
it. The more we exercise any virtue, the more virtuous
we become. Actually, the more we practice virtue, the
more the Holy Spirit works within us, because He is
the embodiment of all virtue; the manifestation of love
in us. *And this is how we know that He lives in us: we
know it by the Spirit He gave us.* (1 John 3:24)

With the desire for a peaceful life comes a desire
for the indwelling Spirit. With the Holy Spirit present
in us we become good as God is good, loving as God
is loving and happy as God is happy. This process of
growth, however, does not happen immediately. The
Holy Spirit starts as a seed and slowly grows and matures in us. He is watered by our prayers, nurtured
by our righteous decisions and fertilized by our good
actions.

Any conversation, situation or problem creates an
opportunity to make a loving decision and a loving action. We are free to make the right or wrong decision,
the good or the evil action. It is usually more difficult
to make the good action, but the Holy Spirit makes it
easier. His presence helps us want what is good and
despise what is evil. For example, if we are in the gro-
cery store and find a wallet on the floor, we may be
tempted to steal it. Our mind will play tricks on us,

trying to convince us of all the reasons why we should keep the wallet. But with the help of the Holy Spirit our conscience will remind us that theft is wrong and will not lead to any lasting benefit. So the Holy Spirit will assist us in making the right decision. His presence will create in us an inclination for good and an aversion toward evil. The more we conform to Him, the easier good actions become. Correct decisions and good actions become less troublesome, because each time we choose rightly, the Holy Spirit grows more in us. Thus goodness matures in us, increasing our ability to love. **And the further we progress in love, the happier we become.**

7

FINDING A NEW FRIEND

I finally made it to high school where I thought my friends were smarter than my parents. My parents told me that smoking and drinking were bad. They acted like they knew what they were talking about. But my friends and I knew what was cool and it was better to be popular than good. I was soon well known because I was cool. I learned how to smoke and drink as well as anyone in school and that is what made me "cool." But then something happened: I got caught. I needed some help, and fast.

I needed my friends to help me out but they were nowhere around. Of all the friends I thought of, not one of them was available to help. The only ones who fully supported me were my parents. They were always ready and willing to help me — they were my true friends. Loyalty, commitment and strength is really what we need. So where can we find these qualities? Who is really our friend?

JESUS OUR FRIEND

What an incredible gift, that Jesus Christ, the King of the universe, wants to be our friend. He oversees everything: from the genes and chromosomes to the plants and animals; from the vapors and gases to the mists and clouds; and from the planets and stars to the solar systems and galaxies and all things in between. He is the cause of the sunrise and sunset, radiating them in His beauty. He is the clothier of the trees and flowers, embracing them in His elegance. He is the spark of life in all beings, empowering them with His love. Jesus is the Person through whom all things were made, and He is in charge of them forever. *"The Father loves the Son and has placed everything in His hands."* (John 3:35) With all this power entrusted to Him, Jesus can have whatever He wants, and what He wants most is love. He declares that love is friendship and He desires to share it with us. *"Greater love has no one than this, that He lay down His life for His friends. You are My friends if you do what I command. I no longer call you servants, because a servant does not know his master's business. Instead, I have called you friends, for everything that I learned from my Father I have made known to you."* (John 15:13)

How lucky we are, how grateful we should be! The greatest Person in the entire universe wants to be our friend. He desires to share His love completely and asks us to be His brother. Jesus invites us to join His family to dwell with Him now and forever. *Pointing to His disciples He said, "Here are My mother and My brothers. For whoever does the will of My Father in heaven is My brother and sister and mother."* (Matthew 12:49)

Because of our human tendency to shun what is available and free, all of us take Him for granted to some degree. When offered a gift that is always accessible but requires a little effort, we don't always accept the gift with our full attention. The King of the universe is certainly worthy of our full attention and deserving of our best effort. But this understanding and desire for Jesus is not immediately clear. First we need to make an effort to learn about Him. **When we open our minds to learn about Jesus, He comes to our hearts that we may know Him.** Then we begin to appreciate Jesus by realizing the treasure He offers in Himself — His friendship. *"For where your treasure is, there your heart will be also."* (Matthew 6:21)

When we truly know Jesus, we can unselfishly desire His friendship with appreciation and gratitude. And until we start sincerely loving, we may desire Him in another way. In the beginning of our relationship we naturally desire Jesus because of the wonderful promises He gives to help and comfort us here on earth. *"Come to Me, all you who are weary and burdened, and I will give you rest. Take My yoke upon you and learn from Me, for I am humble and gentle in heart, and you will find rest for your souls. For My yoke is easy and My burden is light."* (Matthew 11:28) Jesus knows that this world is difficult, that we have frustrations, disappointments, and troubles. He knows that we struggle to survive. He knows that we get sick and that we suffer all types of pain. These are some of the reasons why He wants to help us, to ease our burden and to give us peace. Jesus loves us. He cares about us and makes efforts toward our physical and spiritual wellbeing.

Think of some friends that you truly love. If you saw them in pain, wouldn't you try to help? While they are experiencing grief, doesn't your heart reach out to them? If we truly love someone who is in pain, our reaction is to comfort that person regardless of the effort it demands. That is how Jesus feels about us. He realizes our present and future pain and would do anything for us to relieve it, but He needs our co-operation. A friendship takes at least two persons. So Jesus remains attentive to us, waiting for us to turn to Him that He might give us peace. *"I have told you these things, so that in me you may have peace. In this world you will have trouble. But take heart! I have overcome the world."* (John 16:33)

We all experience times of loneliness and boredom. These feelings are uncomfortable, and often cause us to do things that we later regret. For example: a lonely teenager may reach out for alcohol, drugs or sex, not giving much thought to the action, but seeking the quickest apparent relief. Most of us seek a quick remedy and frequently attempt to relieve our discomfort with irrational behavior. When this occurs, our loneliness may subside for a moment, but soon afterward we feel as lonely as when we started. Boredom operates the same way. Our discomfort with boredom may instigate an action which results in a problem.

But when we become friends with Jesus, we never have to be lonely or bored again. Loneliness and boredom are not part of Jesus, and when we share a relationship with Him, we not only share love, but life — His life. Jesus is with us all the time. We can talk to Him, listen to Him, work with Him, play with Him or pray with Him anytime. Anything we can do spiritually with another person, we can do with Jesus. And He is accessible anytime we want Him and anywhere we need Him.

Jesus Christ is real and His love is within our reach. Be assured that even though we may not see Him, we are capable of feeling Him. When we desire Jesus and ask Him to befriend us, He begins to make His presence known within us. Jesus allows us to detect Him in spiritual, intellectual and physical ways. As we grow closer to Him, we become more aware of His presence. As we continue to love Him by praying to Him and following His commands, Jesus increases our faith. He gives us a heightened awareness of His existence, goodness, truth and beauty. *"Whoever has My commands and obeys them, he is the one who loves Me. He who loves Me will be loved by My Father, and I too will love him and show Myself to Him."* (John 14:21; emphasis added).

Jesus' love then generates a warm peaceful feeling. He comforts us in unspeakable portions that never cease. **Life with Jesus is a fantastic romance: a loving** relationship with the King of all kings; never lonely, never boring and never ending. Unfortunately, we usually concern ourselves only with what we can physically see, and we believe only what we can touch. So most people miss the greatest gift ever: the friendship of Jesus. It helps to humble ourselves and admit that we don't know everything. Then we can be open to receive a deeper faith.

We need to subdue our doubts and consider the existence of God. In recognizing this great opportunity we can turn off our exterior senses in order to concentrate with our interior spirit and ask Jesus to be our friend. This request is an ideal prayer because it sprouts from humility and stems from the heart. Turning away from the world around us enables our mind to break free while allowing our heart to reach forth toward the fulfilling love of Christ. When we initiate this effort, Jesus surprises us with a generous response: the start of our new friendship; the beginning of love in us. We may or may not be awestruck by an overwhelming spiritual experience. However, Jesus will surely bless us with a freshly budding peace, soon to blossom into happiness, later to flourish into everlasting joy. *"My Father will give you whatever you ask in my name. Until now you have not asked for anything in my name. Ask and you will receive, and your joy will be complete."* (John 16:24)

8

INHERITING A GENEROUS MOTHER

During my high school years, I frequently used the word mother, but usually to swear at someone. It seemed that everyone did this so I thought it was normal. When someone crossed me or made me mad, I would curse their mother. I didn't know what I was doing. I didn't know the respect due all mothers. I didn't realize that the most important love is the love of a mother.

Not many people understand the significance and dignity of motherhood. Many modern-day mothers themselves don't appreciate the importance of their role. What is so important about a mother? What is the assistance she gives?

OUR MOTHER MARY

Jesus loves us so much that He gives us His own Holy Mother, the Blessed Virgin Mary, Our Lady of Peace. Jesus is aware of our quest to discover true love in this world and He knows of our difficulty in finding true peace. He understands that real joy comes from divine love. He therefore makes available to us every possible assistance. Jesus was raised and nurtured by the most humble and selfless woman ever born: His Holy Mother, Mary. He gives her to us so that we too may be cared for by such a loving companion. Through God's grace, Mary loves us as her own, completely and unsparingly. *When Jesus saw His mother there, and the disciple whom He loved standing nearby, He said to His mother, "Dear woman, here is your son," and to the disciple, "Here is your mother."* (John 19:26)

There is nothing Mary will not do for us, provided it is for our good. We can ask our mother for help in problems, fears, or rejections. We will never endure any grief that cannot be soothed by our mother's love, with the healing power of our Father's grace. We will never encounter a snare that cannot be untangled by our Mother's intuition, with the wisdom of our brother Jesus. We will never become so lonely that we cannot be reached by our mother's call, with the voice of the Holy Spirit. We never have to worry or be distressed because we have a maternal promise of continuous support. As our Blessed Mother said to Juan Diego at

Mount Tepeyac in Mexico, she says to all of us: *"My little son, do not be distressed and afraid. Am I not here who am your mother? Are you not under my shadow and protection?"*

Mary is always available to us for consolation, to answer our needs and to comfort us. Through our sorrowful and lonely times, our compassionate mother wants us to ask her for love and support. She seeks our attention and waits patiently for us to recognize her presence. She desires our veneration and humble requests to obtain the divine grace we so desperately need. Our most beautiful and pleasing mother Mary now dwells in the merciful heart of Jesus. She waits for our requests, wanting to help us with the power of God. She yearns for our love as a natural mother longs to embrace a wayward child. The promise she made to Juan Diego, in the year 1531, she makes to us all today: *"I will give motherly love and compassion to all who seek my aid."*

We will never grow too big or too old for this gift of maternal care. Our Blessed Mother was created by God, perfect in all ways, never touched by the stain of sin. Our God, Who is perfect, chose to accomplish perfection in Mary, who is the new Eve; the mother of all predestined souls; the mother of the New Covenant, Jesus Christ. Jesus chose to reach us through Mary's most admirable and sacred body, delighting in the affection He found there. He didn't have to enter the world through Mary — He is God. Jesus could have come to the earth in any way He wished. But Jesus accepted His Incarnation within the womb of Mary. He did not consider Himself too great to entrust His life to our Blessed Mother. We should then do likewise with Christ as our model. We can please our Savior by approaching Him along the same path that He chose to come to us, through our same Holy Mother. We will never be rejected or disappointed, for as a mother hen will never leave her chick, our mother Mary will never leave our side. What lost and terrified youngster, who is separated from his mother, will not receive a consoling embrace upon his discovery? And what injured child will not find sympathy and medical aid from his tender mother? So shall we receive kindness and compassion whenever we request it from our precious Mother.

Let us not be afraid to give our attention to Jesus through Mary. Let us not worry that our prayers will fade. And let us never think that our Christian love for Jesus will be misdirected. Mary gave her entire self to Jesus, every day of her life on earth. She certainly wouldn't keep anything for herself now that she is in heaven. She continues to convey to Him all of our intentions. Mary never hinders our way to the Father, rather opens His heart through the Way. *"I am the Way and the Truth and the Life. No one comes to the Father except through Me."* (John 14:6)

Let us follow the example set at the wedding feast at Cana. Mary heard about a problem and she petitioned

Jesus for His help. Jesus quickly resolved the problem, for such an abundantly loving Son can never deny the request of His Mother. *When the wine was gone, Jesus' mother said to Him, "They have no more wine." "Dear woman, why do you involve me?" Jesus replied. "My time has not yet come." His mother said to the servants, "Do whatever He tells you." Nearby stood six stone water jars, the kind used by the Jews for ceremonial washing, each holding from twenty to thirty gallons. Jesus said to the servants, "Fill the jars with water"; so they filled them to the brim. Then he told them, "Now draw some out and take it to the master of the banquet." They did so, and the master of the banquet tasted the water that had been turned into wine.* (John 2:3–9) This account shows the immediate results afforded wise children who seek the remedy, comfort, virtue or strength of Jesus — through the loving hands of Mary.

The wine that ran out, which was replenished by Jesus, can represent our depletion of human energy when faced with too many problems. When our difficulties become overwhelming, they exhaust our limited powers and cause despair. This miserable condition can only be cured through the grace of God. *The Lord gives strength to His people; the Lord blesses His people with peace.* (Psalm 29:11) We are all offered this strength from Jesus, whenever we want it and however we need it. It is most effectively obtained when humbly requested from our loving mother, Mary, the Queen of Peace.

I have come to tell the world that God is truth; He exists. True happiness and the fullness of life are in Him. I have come here as Queen of Peace to tell the world that peace is necessary for the salvation of the world. In God, one finds true joy from which true peace is derived. ["Words From Heaven" — Messages of Our Lady from Medjugorje]

9

ACQUIRING TRUE CONFIDENCE

Upon graduating from high school, I developed a whole new attitude: arrogance. After being a big fish in the little pond of high school, I had a new sense of myself — my ego. Why would I ever need God? Why should I follow any rules? I'm now the captain of my own ship, the king of my own castle. I became proud and self-centered. But after starting college I changed. It didn't take long for me to realize that I was just a little boy in a whole new world. My confidence stemmed from pride without God's strength and support. So after a few minor failures, I shrank down below adequate size to an incomplete ego. Within the first year my sense of self-worth vanished.

Pleasure became my ego booster, reducing my self-esteem further. My confident appearance was only a mask hiding my fear of failure. I pretended that all was fine when actually I was hurting inside. The cure for that pain is confidence. So where does true confidence come from? How and where can we get it?

PERSONAL DIGNITY

God created each of us in His image. *So God created man in His image; in the image of God He created him; male and female He created them.* (Genesis 1:27) Each one of us has been made distinctly unique. God loves us all and He loves each one of us as the only one of our kind, rare and precious. **We are each more prized than anything else and each more cherished than all things combined.** *God blessed them and said to them, "Be fruitful and multiply, fill the earth and subdue it, rule over the fish of the sea and the birds of the sky, over every living creature that moves on the ground."* (Genesis 1:28)

There is dignity in this knowledge; confidence in God with this truth. We benefit from this understanding because it generates the fortitude we need for survival. This sense of self-worth becomes the primary force in us. It propels our will to live and motivates us to act. Awareness of God's existence allows the formation of self-esteem, a love of self that is rightly ordered when we humbly recognize God's love for us. But opposed to self-esteem is self-pride which generates a false confidence. Pride by itself leads away from true faith and directs all belief and trust back to ourselves. Let us be confident in God, rather than in ourselves. Let us put our trust in God. After all, He is the One Who made us. He preserves us in life and participates in every breath we take.

Why do we not consider God worthy of our trust? Why would He carefully design every detail and create such a beautiful planet for us if He didn't desire our well-being? God created an extraordinary world with an extensive assortment of food and provisions because He cares for us. He loves us and wants the best for us. To further demonstrate His readiness to help us, God the Father sent His Son, that we may witness His genuine love and thereby trust Him fully. Never before in the history of the world has such love been seen. Yet we behave as if God doesn't care. When we lose our confidence in God and place it all in ourselves, we are acting as if He is not worthy of our trust. Yet God, the Divine Being, Who made the earth and all its surroundings from absolutely nothing, can easily solve our problems. He is certainly more capable than we are to provide for our needs and resolve our troubles. *"Do not let your hearts be troubled. Trust in God."* (John 14:1)

Then why do we place so little trust in God and so much confidence in ourselves? Because of our lack of understanding and our lack of faith. We need to ask God to help us believe before we can learn to trust. *"But if You can do anything, take pity on us and help us." "If you can?" said Jesus. "Everything is possible for him who believes." Immediately the boy's father exclaimed, "I do believe; help my unbelief!"* (Mark 9:22–24)

To fully trust God, we must have faith in the existence, goodness, truth, and beauty of our most gracious God; our most generous Benefactor. *"Now this is eternal life: that they may know (believe) You, the only true God, and Jesus Christ, whom You have sent."* (John 17:3)

We learn to place our full confidence in God when we comprehend His Gospel message. *"I have come that you may have life, and have it to the full."* (John 10:10)

To develop a stronger belief in God, ask for faith and you will receive it. To establish a greater trust in God, seek for hope and you shall find it. To possess the resulting love in God, knock at the door of charity and it will be opened to you. *"For everyone who asks receives; he who seeks, finds; and to him who knocks, the door will be opened."* (Matthew 7:8) To achieve growth in virtue, think, act and pray according to the counsel of the saints — humility, humility, humility. *"For whoever exalts himself will be humbled, and whoever humbles himself will be exalted."* (Matthew 23:11) To receive the confidence in God that brings us peace through any catastrophe, begin to pray with humility, the foundation of all virtue. *This poor [humble] man called, and the Lord heard him; He saved Him out of all his troubles.* (Psalm 34:6)

When we realize that God carefully made each one of us and that He dearly loves us as His own, we receive a proper sense of self-worth. This awareness is true confidence because it is found in the truth of faith, maintained by the humility of hope, and sustained by the virtue of love. This sense of self-worth motivates us and establishes our dignity. The personal benefits of this awareness include the elimination of anxiety and fear. How can we fear when we know that God, who can do all things, will help us? David was not frightened when he stood before Goliath, because he was not relying on his own strength but on the power of God. *"The Lord who delivered me from the paw of the lion and the paw of the bear will deliver me from the hand of this Philistine."* (1 Samuel 17:37)

Those of us who experience impatience and frustration can benefit from a greater faith and trust in God. Consider a student who frantically takes an exam when the unexpected bell announces that the time limit is quickly approaching. Imagine a homemaker who hurriedly makes dinner for her soon to return spouse, when the infant starts crying and the toddler spills juice on the carpet. Any situation like this can cause anxiety and frustration if we forget that God is with us. We sometimes think that we have to solve all of our problems by ourselves. But we don't have to solve them alone and we don't have to suffer through stress because God will always assist us. And our Friend, Jesus, Who provides the solution comes through the indwelling Spirit. And the Holy Spirit helps us to accept the outcome peacefully. *"I have told you these things so that in me you may have peace. In this world you will have trouble. But take heart! I have overcome the world."* (John 16:33)

Psychologists agree on four basic human fears: rejection, failure, suffering and death. These fears generate nervousness and anxiety. As our relationship with God develops so does our trust in Him. The results of this new partnership include a more constant awareness of His presence and a greater knowledge of His help. **As our friendship with God strengthens, our natural fears weaken.** We can overcome all of these fears by our thorough understanding of God's existence within us. We can never be totally rejected because God is present within us and He loves us more than anyone in this world. We can never totally fail because God is successful in us and He enjoys our success in love more than anything in this world. We can never totally suffer because God is strength in us and He sustains us throughout any hardship in this world. And we can never totally die because God dwells within us and He maintains us in life after this world. *"I have given them the glory that You gave Me, that they may be one as We are one: I in them and You in Me. May they be brought to complete unity to let the world know that You sent me and have loved them even as You have loved Me."* (John 17:22–23)

By believing and trusting in God, we also eliminate our everyday worries. **With God there is nothing to worry about because He will always help us.** *"Therefore I tell you, do not worry about your life, what you will eat or what you will drink; or about your body, what you will wear. Is not life more important than food, and the body more important than clothes? Look at the birds of the air; they do not sow or reap or store away in barns, and yet your heavenly Father feeds them. Are you not much more valuable than they? Who of you by worrying can add a single hour to his life? And why do you worry about clothes? See how the lilies of the field grow. They do not labor or spin. Yet I tell you that not even Solomon in all his splendor was dressed like one of these. If that is how God clothes the grass of the field, which* is here today and tomorrow is thrown into the fire, will He not much more clothe you, O you of little faith? So do not worry, saying, 'What shall we eat?' or 'What shall we drink?' or 'What shall we wear?' For the pagans run after all these things, and your heavenly Father knows that you need them. But seek first His kingdom and His righteousness, and all these things will be given you as well. Therefore do not worry about tomorrow, for tomorrow will worry about itself. Each day has enough trouble of its own. (Matthew 6:25–34)

10

GROWING BEYOND GUILT

The wave of "fun" at college soon caught up and overtook me. I was like a surfer who glides for too long, thinking the ride will never end. So I came crashing down with the curl upon the rocky reef. As the rolling and rising water sucks up all that is around it, my wave of pleasure engulfed all duties, absorbing them into my passions. I slept in the bed of iniquity, dreaming with sensuality and pleasure, asleep to the reality of my college education and dead to the Truth of God.

During my senior year I temporarily awoke. While becoming aware of my past, I started drowning in regret. I felt ashamed and guilty and began to despair over the seemingly impossible escape. Thinking I was all alone, I soon tried to change by myself. But guilt is like quicksand — it requires help to pull free. So as I wrestled with it alone, temptations grew ever stronger, and the more I struggled the more I sinned. I began to sink deeper in guilt, wondering how I had sunk so low. How can we avoid the horrors of shame? And how can we grow beyond guilt?

ACCEPTING GOD'S WILL

We tend to believe that we control all the events around us. We generally want to manipulate all of the circumstances in which we live rather than accept them as they are. This behavior is considered normal as most of us would agree that if we do not like the heat, we should not live in the desert. We choose where we want to live. And if we do not like the cold, then we should not work in the snow. We are likewise free to choose where we work. These choices are obviously acceptable and important to decide. But somewhere along our journey of life, we attempt to expand our dominion into areas beyond our control. We sometimes blame ourselves for bad things that happen to us that are governed by chance.

Whenever our life does not happen as planned, we are usually quick to blame someone, even though that someone is frequently our own self. We sometimes act as if we control all the circumstances along the way. For example, if we drive to work, many unforeseen delays are possible. We could be stopped in a traffic jam because of an accident on the road. Unsolicited thoughts then start to appear in our minds. "Why did I miss the traffic report? I never miss it, and now when I needed to hear it, I didn't. What a dummy." Or . . . "Why did I have to go this way? I never use this road, and now, when I've got to be at work early, I use it and get stuck." When we think that we control the whole of our life, we cause ourselves needless problems. We disrupt our own peace.

Think about a person who has prepared for an important meeting which will determine his salary for the next two years. Weeks of work have been spent preparing and reviewing documentation of past achievements. Finally he is ready for the big meeting and on the drive to work, everything appears to be smooth, then *"blam!"*: the front right tire blows out and his car skids off the road. Despite a nearby telephone, his immediate reaction is a combination of frustration, anger, disappointment, and guilt.

We subject ourselves to anxiety in situations when a bad thing happens. We suffer needlessly without an awareness of God's will. What we don't see and therefore avoid, God sees for us. In the above incident the person would have hit a truck at the following intersection, thus meeting with a premature death. God alone knows our highest good. He never allows an event to part from His plan for our salvation, and with it our eternal happiness.

God's plan? God's will? What about our free will? Indeed we have our own free will and God will not take it away from us. There is, however, the supernatural blessing of divine intervention. God interacts with our free will in a mysterious fashion. Recognizing God's interaction is necessary for us to enjoy a carefree life. God cares what happens to us here and participates in our daily life. God answers every prayer.

Sometimes He says, "yes," and implements an action. Sometimes He says, "no," with a corresponding inaction. And sometimes He says, "not now, maybe later." *I sought the Lord, and He answered me; He delivered me from all my fears.* (Psalm 34:4)

God communicates His designs to us frequently and in various ways. But most of us seldom hear Him because we are not attuned to His voice. **We listen to God with our hearts and therefore need humility to hear Him.** We demonstrate our love for God and become aware of His will when we respond to His request of loving each other. *"Lord, when did we see You hungry and feed You, or thirsty and give You something to drink? When did we see You a stranger and invite You in, or needing clothes and clothe You? When did we see You sick or in prison and go and visit You?"* . . . *"I tell you the truth, whatever you did for one of the least of these brothers of mine, you did for Me."* (Matthew 25:37–40)

The Old Testament is filled with examples of God speaking to people, but in the New Testament, God communicates everything in just one Word. That Word is *Jesus*, which literally means "God saves." Along with the Word comes all that He did, summarized in one simple message: love. If we live in humility, the beginning of all virtue, we live in the light of understanding and can thereby hear God's voice. Then we can know and perform God's will and gain everlasting life. If we live in pride, the root of all evil, we live in darkness. There we neither understand love nor participate in it.

In the beginning was the Word, and the Word was with God, and the Word was God. He was with God in the beginning. Through Him all things were made; without Him nothing was made. In Him was life, and that life was the light of men. The light shines in the darkness, but the darkness has not understood it. (John 1:1–5)

When we accept God's will, we accept God's love. And when we accept Love, we accept God Himself. We are free to try to control everything in our "own little universe," but with that attempt come frustration, disappointment, worry, and guilt. But when we trust God with our life we give the control to Him. We are then released from these anxieties and receive true freedom. We live in God's love which enables us to live care-free because we know that God will always help us. We allow our Father to control our lives and we bestow total confidence in Him as we trust in His goodness. *"Which of you fathers, if your son asks for a fish, will give him a snake instead? Or if he asks for an egg, will give him a scorpion? If you then, though you are imperfect, know how to give good gifts to your children, how much more will your Father in heaven give to those who ask Him!"* (Luke 11:11)

When we surrender ourselves to God, we become liberated from worry and guilt. *Even though I walk through the valley of the shadow of death, I will fear no evil, for You are with me.* (Psalm 23:4) **With complete trust in God we always know that whatever happens is for our highest good.** Our highest good is to be with

God in heaven some day. Everything that happens to us is allowed by God to achieve this end — our eternal happiness. Even when we make a mistake, it is allowed by God for a higher good. *And we know that in all things God works for the good of those who love Him.* (Romans 8:28) So we don't have to worry about the future, and we never regret the past. All that remains is for us to enjoy our daily gift from God — "the present."

11

OBTAINING HELP FOR OUR PROBLEMS

I thought I had problems at the beginning of college but those were nothing compared to the end. I was expected to graduate on time but my extra-curricular, illicit activities put me far behind schedule. To complete my final semester, I had more classes remaining than I was allowed to take. There was no natural hope for me to graduate on time so I asked God for His supernatural help.

I had eleven classes left, totaling thirty-one course units; double the normal student load. God helped me to make a start by giving me confidence in Him. He then provided the classes by making them all available. He enabled me to get permission to take them all at once. He proceeded to walk me through the ordeal, continuing His help at each turn. There were many all-night study sessions, three and four tests on some days, and personal hardships of every kind. At the end there were two final exams scheduled for the same period. But I persisted with confidence in God and finally finished.

God's intervention helped me complete the impossible dream. Those events at college made me understand that God listens to us and wants to solve our problems with our participation.

So how does He work with us?

DIVINE INTERVENTION

When we begin to believe in God, we start to recognize divine actions which affect our everyday life. God allows us to witness His actions to reinforce our faith. This usually happens with problems when we understand that the outcomes did not just happen by our own efforts or by mere circumstance. We receive from God an awareness of His presence with an undoubtable knowledge of His supernatural involvement. **These heavenly favors are called divine intervention and bless our lives with increased faith, revitalized hope, and enhanced charity.** *You prepare a table before me in the presence of my enemies. You anoint my head with oil; my cup overflows.* (Psalm 23:5) However, not all of our problems are solved with such effective solutions and beneficial results. And some of our dilemmas remain unresolved. To understand the reasons why God allows these trials and disappointments, let us first review the methods of His assistance. God teaches us how to live through His commands of how to love. He then guides us through our troubles with patience and trust in Him. And finally, God encourages us to overcome our weaknesses through situations that exercise virtue.

The biggest problems in the world and likewise our personal difficulties persist because of a lack of love. There would not be people lacking food if the gluttonous multitude of the world spared just one of their daily appetizers. There would not be people without clothes if the ostentatious majority of this world provided just one of their least favored outfits. There would not be people without homes if the mansion dwelling masses of the world furnished just one of their littlest rooms. When we recognize the vast wealth on our planet in contrast to the unnecessary affliction that so many people endure, we have identified the current injustice. This situation will only improve when together we follow the teaching of Jesus. *Then the King will say to those on His right, "Come, you who are blessed by my Father; take your inheritance, the kingdom prepared for you since the creation of the world. For I was hungry and you gave me something to eat, I was thirsty and you gave me something to drink, I was a stranger and you invited me in, I needed clothes and you clothed me, I was sick and you looked after me, I was in prison and you came to visit me."* (Matthew 25:34–36)

Most of our relationship problems stem from our disobedience of God's commands and a lack of charity (love) for our neighbors. Thus, we should analyze our troubles, first from our own shortcomings rather than those of others. *"Why do you look at the speck of sawdust in your brother's eye and pay no attention to the plank in your own eye? . . . first take the plank out of your own eye, and then you will see clearly to remove the speck from your brother's eye."* (Matthew 7:3–5) When we look inside ourselves first, we can usually pinpoint the source of our trouble and then correct it with the blessings of God. If we discover that a part of our problem is caused by someone else, we are then illumined and capable of discussing it with that person without confusion. We can then solve our relationship problems with the grace of God and the teachings of love. *"If your brother sins against you, go and show him his fault, just between the two of you. If he listens to you, you have won your brother over."* (Matthew 18:15)

Sometimes we encounter predicaments that are emotionally overwhelming. Our whole life appears connected to the problem and we can't concentrate on anything else. We actually become obsessed with the situation which then hinders all other activities. Our once peaceful and attractive demeanor becomes rash and repulsive. When this condition is prolonged, originally supportive friends become annoyed by our constant complaining. What started as a single problem becomes an entanglement of troubles that consumes our personality and afflicts our entire being. The difficulty now seems larger than life because we are too upset to realize that God *is* life and certainly greater than any of our troubles. **With a spiritual perspective we realize that any problem we have can only be as big as we make it.** But in our lack of patience and trust in God, we make mountains out of mole hills. Then the only solution is peaceful prayer to reunite ourselves with our Protector to ask for His assistance. And comfort He will give, coming speedily to our aid — for no Father will reject the humble cry of His own. Our prayer will yield peace from God, allowing us clarity in reviewing our options. Then confidence in God will generate a new inner strength that will help us work through the problem. And soon after starting the effort God returns our joy to us. *Hear, O Lord, and be merciful to me; O Lord, be my help. You turned my wailing into dancing; You removed my sackcloth and clothed me with joy.* (Psalm 30:10–11)

Our God has made us to be His children and thereby enjoy His benefits. Because of His goodness, God gave us free will and the ability to accept Him as our Father. When we decide to accept God, we need to strengthen that decision by exercising trust. We thus communicate our faith to Him and then share in the resulting hope of His promises. This brings forth the mercy of God and prompts His assistance to our everyday needs. *Yet to all who received Him, to those who believed in His name, He gave the right to become children of God — children born not of natural descent, nor of human decision or a husband's will, but born of God.* (John 1:12–13)

This help we receive from God includes the benefits necessary for our happiness starting with faith, hope and charity. His gifts continue next with humility, appreciation and gratitude, which open the gateway to advanced levels of patience, gentleness, and tranquility. God's offerings progress to caring, kindness and compassion which promote understanding, forgiveness and peace. We need true love and trust in God to receive these supernatural gifts because a mighty effort is required to attain them. **It is necessary to realize the importance of love so that we can increase**

our desire for it. *"Whoever has will be given more. . . ."* (Luke 8:18)

When we are accustomed to eating three meals per day and then do not eat for several days, we sincerely appreciate food and will stop at nothing to obtain it. Likewise, when we are surrounded by love every day and then don't receive it for several days, we become aware of the necessity of love and yearn for its fulfillment. Consider a time when a loved one had to travel away for a long time. Did you miss that person and hope for an expedient return? Also, trust in God's love initiates a joyful longing to dwell with Him. *"The kingdom of heaven is like treasure hidden in a field. When a man found it, he hid it again, and then in his joy went and sold all he had and bought that field. Again the kingdom of heaven is like a merchant looking for fine pearls. When he found one of great value, he went away and sold everything he had and bought it."* (Matthew 13:44–46)

God is ready, willing and able to give us His love which we need for our peace and continuing happiness. We need to establish a burning desire for this love because it comes mostly through the problems that we encounter. All dilemmas are opportunities to grow in love. God alone knows what will help us and He allows certain problems to trouble the weaker parts of our character to form us into beings of love. When our strongest desire is to grow in love and thus to be with God, we no longer complain about the problems we encounter, but rather thank God for allowing them to occur. We recognize that God will work with us to solve the problem while exercising a flaw in our character to help us mature.

God is the heavenly potter, Who molds us (the clay) into the image of His Son, Jesus Christ. We can picture clay spinning around on a wheel, pulled out in one place for patience, pushed in another for caring and trimmed at the top to cut back our arrogance. *"Yet, O Lord, You are our Father. We are the clay, You are the potter; we are all the work of Your hand."* (Isaiah 64:8) Learning can be difficult and spiritual growth can be troublesome. But let us have confidence in God, because He helps us solve our problems while forming the masterpieces of love that we are each created to be.

12

ENJOYING
MEANINGFUL RELATIONSHIPS

I have heard people say how much they loved college. I have heard it described as the best time of life and a place to establish friendships. But I didn't make many friends there. Most people seemed shallow to me because I was shallow to them. I didn't care much about people in college, I was preoccupied with myself and my worries. College presented a unique opportunity to meet people and get to know them. It is a shame that I did not participate. I met many good people and had plenty of conversations but generally remained indifferent. We studied together and went out together yet I never got to know anyone well.

But other people seemed to get close. I noticed many friendships that were loyal and true. So what was I doing wrong? How do we become closer friends?

FULFILLING FRIENDSHIPS

We enjoy close friendships through God's love, for He contains all the meaning of life. Consider an extended family gathered together for a reunion in a park. The sun is up and the wind is down; the barbecue is smoking and recreation abounds. Sounds of children at play blend with the cultural music of old days. There are grandfathers and grandmothers, husbands and wives, teenagers and youngsters all merrily alive. They are involved in sports, games, and conversations and while each activity generates pleasure, there exists a deeper joy in the people. They rejoice in the union of family and concern themselves first with each other. Their bright smiling faces expose an outpouring of inner delight, stimulated by the excitement of sharing with each other. Their enjoyment comes from the fulfilling happiness of the love of God. These people are not relying on worldly pleasure for their joy. Instead, they are jubilant with the simple expressions of familial bonds. They are unified by God, which intensifies their care for each other in this loving moment of life. **Their happiness originates from genuine love, given by our Father above.** *Dear friends, let us love one another, for love comes from God.* (1 John 4:7)

Sometimes however, relationships can be based on utility rather than love. This exists when one of the parties cares less about the other person and more about what they might get from the relationship. This fellowship is based on selfish interests and is therefore not a true friendship. It is more like a person's connection with a disposable fork or spoon. The only concern about the utensil is the service it provides, and when the service is over the tool is then thrown away. Unfortunately, this kind of human relationship is so common that most of us, at one time or another, have experienced the feeling of having been used. Emotional turmoil results when it occurs in a serious relationship. Sometimes we sense mutual love with someone, but are disappointed by their constant interest in getting what we have, rather than accepting who we are. And sometimes when our usefulness to someone ends, they abruptly end the relationship. *Now on His way to Jerusalem, Jesus traveled along the border between Samaria and Galilee. As He was going into a village, ten men who had leprosy met Him. They stood at a distance and called out in a loud voice, "Jesus, Master, have pity on us!" When He saw them, He said, "Go, show yourselves to the priests." And as they went, they were cleansed. One of them, when he saw he was healed, came back, praising God in a loud voice. He threw himself at Jesus' feet and thanked Him — and he was a Samaritan. Jesus asked, "Were not all ten cleansed? Where are the other nine? Was no one found to return and give praise to God except this foreigner?"* (Luke 17:11–18)

Jesus knows about human anguish brought about by one-way love. But that did not stop Him from searching for honesty, and teaching us the way to gain it. He exemplifies pure love which generates sincerity, that in turn creates the happiness of God. Actually,

Jesus is so abundantly filled with love, that He stops at nothing to communicate its joy — not even His own suffering and death. *And being found in appearance as a man, he humbled Himself and became obedient unto death — even death on a cross!* (Philippians 2:8)

To understand the fulfilling happiness we enjoy from relationships found in God's love, we can all compare the variety of friendships we have already experienced. Let us first recall our more distant associations and reflect on the reasons for their emptiness. They might have been connections from business which served only a temporary purpose, and then terminated upon the completion of the job. These encounters remain shallow when the participants place more value on compensation than the fellowship involved. We cannot expect real love to develop from affiliations based on money or materials. *"No one can serve two masters. Either he will hate the one and love the other, or he will be devoted to one and despise the other. You cannot serve both God and money."* (Matthew 6:24)

We may not recognize any lack of companionship until a situation tests the friendship. Acquaintances may appear friendly, but we don't actually see their true colors until the opportunity arises. If the association is based on worldly desires it will not survive the trial. If the friendship is grounded in the love of God, the union will not only endure the test, but become stronger because of it. **Relationships initiated and sustained in God's love are like the refiner's metals, pu-**

rified and strengthened by fire. *"I will strengthen you and help you."* (Isaiah 41:10)

These truly honest relationships are more deeply loving than any other, because in such an alliance we are more concerned about our friend's happiness than our own. The majority of actions and teachings in this world give us no reason to care about anyone more than ourselves. There is no worldly explanation for the desire to sacrifice one's own benefit for that of another, yet this is necessary for love. *"Greater love has no one than this, that he lay down his life for his friends."* (John 15:13)

Real love is unselfish, kind, tolerant, generous, understanding, and gentle. This true love and the happiness it generates is not derived from anything on earth, but from our Father in heaven. *And so we know and rely on the love God has for us. God is love. Whoever lives in love lives in God, and God in him.* (1 John 4:16) Everything from this world diminishes as it is used. Earthly resources like oil and coal decrease as they are utilized. Similarly, all things of this world diminish as they are given away. **However, the more love we give, the more love we gain.** If we have two twenty-dollar bills, and we give one of them to a needy person, our worldly possessions decrease, but our heavenly charity increases. The more kind we are, the more caring we become. The more tolerant we are, the more patience we receive. The more generous we are, the more compassion we develop. The more understanding we are, the more forgiveness we acquire. The more gentle we are, the more tranquil we become. When we exercise concern for our neighbor, love matures within us. Our continuing effort to advance God's love generates more deeply loving relationships. **And the more we accomplish God's love with our neighbor, the more peace and joy we experience.** *"Do not judge, and you will not be judged. Do not condemn, and you will not be condemned. Forgive, and you will be forgiven. Give, and it will be given to you. A good measure, pressed down, shaken together and running over, will be poured into your lap. For the measure you use, it will be measured to you."* (Luke 6:37–38)

13

LIVING IN HAPPINESS NOW AND FOREVER

Many people had a great time in college but that was not true for me. My college experience was terrible. I wasn't happy during classes and homework or during most of the parties. There were momentary pleasures, but always coupled with worry or guilt. It seems now like a bad dream, trying to run but slipping and never really moving. Pleasure got closer and closer, the light of God farther away. My personality lost its substance while everything I did was motivated by a desire for fun.

The only time I was happy was during the last semester. Eleven classes and thirty-one units with no time to party — that just doesn't make any sense. With so much work that semester, how could I have been happy? Because I felt close to God. It was then that I gave the most love. But what does love have to do with happiness and how can we live in it now?

LIVING WITH LOVE

The more we give the more we gain. Giving love from us makes more love within us. And the more God's love grows within us the more peaceful and happy we become. *Blessed [happy] are they who follow the law of the Lord.* (Psalm 119:1) *"This is my command [law]: Love each other."* (John 15:17) The degree of our peace depends on the extent of love we maintain. Someone who distributes only a little love will receive only a limited happiness in this world, while someone who contributes much love will correspondingly celebrate exhilarating joy, now on earth and forever in heaven. *"Anyone who receives a prophet because he is a prophet will receive a prophet's reward, and anyone who receives a righteous man because he is a righteous man will receive a righteous man's reward."* (Matthew 10:41) We thus have tremendous incentive to live a charitable life — that we may enjoy the immense tranquility and happiness contained in love's carefree caress. For which one of us has experienced a more satisfying delight than the comfort of knowing that we are loved. **Sometimes we may prefer action and sometimes we favor rest. But at all times it seems that if we could dream, we would ever choose love as the best.**

Then why don't we all love everyone always? Most people don't understand love and therefore don't teach it to others, including their own children. *Can a blind man lead a blind man? Will they not both fall into a pit?* (Luke 6:39) Also, most of us do not yet realize that the key to happiness is love and that true love is found only in God. *He was in the world, and though the world was made through Him, the world did not recognize Him.* (John 1:10) And finally because it is usually difficult to love. *For wide is the gate and broad is the road that leads to destruction, and many enter through it. But small is the gate and narrow the road that leads to life, and only a few find it.* (Matthew 7:13–14)

Let us not get confused between the definition of love and the results of love. The fruits of love are soothing and therefore enjoyable. But the practice of love is difficult and usually requires self-denial for the benefit of others. If a spouse desires to watch baseball it is easy to accommodate a game, especially when the alternative is yard work. But when the request is for cleaning outside, the yard work becomes a loving act, especially when the alternative is baseball. We commonly attribute warm feelings to love itself, but these are results of love as opposed to acts of love.

Love is not a feeling but a decision. Love is an act of the will. To love someone is to treat that person accordingly — as we wish to be treated ourselves. *"Do to others as you would have them do to you."* (Luke 6:31) Consider the mother of a newborn child. The little baby has just spent nine months and a day causing nothing but pain. In the first three months, there was nausea and sickness, in the next three there was constipation and gas. The final term offered a distorted body, and the day of delivery produced incomparable pain. Yet the moment that mother first holds her baby she experiences a peaceful joy. **And therein lies the mystery of love — sacrificing oneself for another results in peace and joy.**

Giving love generates understanding, peace and joy. But the loving efforts of people who walk in the light of God appear worthless to those overshadowed by darkness. *In Him was life, and that life was the light of men. The light shines in the darkness, but the darkness has not understood it.* (John 1:4–5) When we act with love we are donating our energy, time or money for someone else's benefit without any material profit. According to the logic of the world this contribution wastes valuable resources. Before committing to any activity, most people ask, "What is in it for me?" "Look out for number one," demand the counselors of our age.

These attitudes contribute to war, crime and starvation. What a grave misfortune, especially when love will generate happiness. Think of the mother described. This princess of love went through labor and pain yet became the happiest she has ever been. **Any effort given in love always yields peace to the lover.** *Peace I leave with you; my peace I give you.* (John 14:27) And with Christ's peace arrives life's full joy. *I have come that they may have life, and have it to the full.* (John 10:10) And with Christ's joy comes a new understanding of the power of love. *"I am the light of the world. Whoever follows me will never walk in darkness, but will have the light of life."* (John 8:12)

Love can sometimes be difficult to achieve. When we finally discover the truth about love, we have already developed personality traits which require re-training before we can love. Making these changes by following God's advice is arduous and challenging. *"You have heard that it was said, 'Love your neighbor and hate your enemy.' But I tell you: love your enemies and pray for those who persecute you, that you may be sons of your Father in heaven. He causes His sun to rise on the evil and the good, and sends rain on the righteous and the unrighteous. If you love those who love you, what reward will you get? Are not even the tax collectors doing that? And if you greet only your brothers, what are you doing more than others? Do not even the pagans do that? Be perfect therefore, as your heavenly father is perfect."* (Matthew 5:43–48) Yet this work of self-improvement is necessary for a more loving disposition and a happier life. Even though love requires sacrifice, those who love receive the reward promised by Jesus Christ. *"I tell you the truth,"* Jesus replied, *"no one who has left home or brothers or sisters or mother or father or children or fields for Me and the Gospel will fail to receive a hundred times as much in this present age, and in the age to come, eternal life."* (Mark 10:29–30)

DESIRING PEACE
DIVINE MOTIVATIONS

14

GOD'S GREATEST GIFT

After graduating from college, I went on vacation for a few months before starting work in the "real world." I was pleased to be finished with school and thankful to God for His help. I thought about Him often and was grateful for all His assistance. Then I started working and soon became hungry for money and image. Nobody at work ever talked about God, only the gods they had made. Their schedule was god, their money was god, and recreation was god to them. I was too weak to challenge their religion. They were leaders in the world and I wanted to be accepted and liked. I wanted to succeed. I don't think it took more than a month for me to abandon all of my gratitude to God.

To justify my un-Godly desires, I rationalized away the real God. For immediate pleasure and self-gratification I accepted the gods of the world. I was pulled into the modern-day mentality: "I say a prayer before I sleep, that's enough for me." I was spiritually lazy with the flippant attitude, What has God ever done for me?

THE PASSION OF JESUS CHRIST

INTRODUCTION

Through Jesus Christ we were first given life. Due to our disobedience we lost our lives. So the great Redeemer saved our life by giving His own in reparation. When He gave His life by death on the cross, He shared everything with us, even His own Immaculate Mother, Divine Father and Holy Spirit. Jesus gives us everything He has, including His entire Self. These gifts are not free to Him. He gives us divine gifts and they have cost Him a divine price. Each gift is more valuable than anything on earth, and thus commanded a reckoning greater than anything extracted or made from this world.

Jesus wants us to understand how much He loves us, so He accepted a painful death to atone for our sins. The extent to which someone loves can only be recognized through actions, not words. It is easy to say things with good intentions, but only by expending effort do we exhibit love. And to display pure love, the effort must be totally selfless. It is therefore uncommon to give pure love through our normal actions because we usually enjoy the act, making it not totally selfless. If a mother takes her child to a play, she will receive pleasure from the child's enjoyment, even if unintentional. This action certainly displays love. But to demonstrate the purest love possible there must be no trace of the giver's enjoyment.

Pure love can be found in an act of personal suffering where the lover undergoes suffering for the benefit of the beloved. Because Jesus wants us to comprehend His infinite love for us, He accepted an act of infinite suffering. Even though Jesus suffered frustrations and humiliations all His life, reference to His Passion begins in Gethsemane. So let us also start there to identify with Christ's abundant love as evidenced by His supernatural suffering. Words alone will never capture the extent of His effort. Nevertheless, to receive a deeper understanding of Christ's Passion, we should try to imagine ourselves in His place and ask the Holy Spirit for His guidance and grace.

THE AGONY IN THE GARDEN

The night before He was betrayed, Jesus went to the garden of Gethsemane to pray in solitude to God. The Gospel gives us two main elements of Christ's prayer on that night. First, He asked, *"Father, if You are willing, take this cup from Me; yet not My will but Yours be done."* (Luke 22:42) What a beautiful illustration of Jesus' love for His Father. He would consent to His Father's will unto death, even death on a cross. Secondly, He prayed so intensely that *His sweat was like drops of blood, falling to the ground.* (Luke 22:44) Our initial thought might be that Jesus was so disturbed by His impending torture that He consequently sweat blood. However, Jesus was not concerned for Himself but for each one of us.

We must understand that Jesus does not think about all of us as "humankind," rather He thinks of each one of us as individuals. In one moment He intimately knows each individual ever created; past, present and future. When Jesus died for us, it is you and I personally; not us as a collective whole. Jesus gives His life to each one of us independently. So in the garden He thought about each of the souls He was about to save. He also reflected on each of the souls that would not respond to Him and therefore would not be saved. Jesus wanted to save everyone and prayed so intensely for each soul that He sweat drops of blood.

It is a medical fact that our blood gets thinner when we are under duress. It has been proven that a person's blood could become thin enough to weep out of the pores of human skin.

We may now understand the unbearable stress that Christ felt while praying in the garden. His love for us is so great that He cannot bear the thought of losing any one of us. Christ sweat blood — pouring His heart out to God, begging Him to save everyone, even those who choose wickedness. If Jesus so loves an evil person as to actually sweat blood from compassion, then His love for us is inexhaustible — it is truly infinite.

In the early morning, following this night of prayer, a friend came to betray Christ, bringing soldiers to arrest Him. *A crowd came up and the man who was called Judas, one of the Twelve, was leading them. He approached Jesus to kiss Him, but Jesus asked Him, "Judas, are you betraying the Son of man with a kiss?"* (Luke 22:47–48)

Christ's apostles were His best friends and His betrayer was one of the apostles. Can you imagine your best friend betraying you to your death? The pain would be excruciating, far beyond any physical abuse. The extent of that agony would be directly proportional to the degree of love you had for the betrayer. If you didn't really care for the betrayer there would be no real sense of loss felt and therefore no grief or emptiness. However, if you loved that person, then the betrayal would cause overwhelming pain. We know that Jesus' love is infinite so His anguish from this betrayal was infinitely agonizing.

The soldiers took Jesus along a path through the walls of Jerusalem to a small room with a stone floor. Upon entering the barren cell, a guard struck Him on the face and they all joined in, hitting and jeering without remorse. *The men who were guarding Jesus began mocking and beating Him. They blindfolded Him and demanded, "Prophesy! Who hit You?" And they said many other insulting things to Him.* (Luke 22:63–65)

The soldiers finally left and Jesus remained there alone. Now in that dim room, no cot was present and no comfort was to be found. Jesus sat on a rock, waiting for His doom. He was hungry and cold. Jesus sat there shivering, knowing that on earth He would never be relieved, but would only receive added injuries in overwhelming degrees. *He was despised and rejected by men, a man of sorrows and familiar with suffering.* (Isaiah 53:3)

THE SCOURGING AT THE PILLAR

After the rising of the sun, the soldiers came in and jolted Christ, bound Him and dragged Him out to trial. He stood in a room with several officers and a ruler named Pontius Pilate. Throughout the city, news of the arrest had spread, and many people started gathering outside. Pilate began asking questions, but it all seemed ridiculous. Who is this arrogant man who questions our God? And Jesus didn't cause any trouble but remained gentle and humble. When Pilate could find no reason to sentence Jesus, he walked outside and said to the people, "I find no case against Him. What will you have me do?" Jesus could hear the people yelling, "Crucify Him." Then Pilate responded, *"Why? What crime has He committed?" . . . But they shouted all the louder, "Crucify Him!"* (Mark 15:14) After He spent His life for them (the last three years of which included walking down hot dusty roads — teaching, feeding, and healing them) again the betrayal resounded. Christ's people only wished to see Him suffer pain and death. Pilate was then pressured to make a decision. Not knowing what to do, he decided to satisfy the crowd. *He had Jesus flogged, and handed Him over to be crucified.* (Mark 15:15)

The soldiers then dragged Jesus away and tied him up, facing a pole. They proceeded to strike His back with whips. These were no ordinary straps but devices designed to rip the skin and gouge the flesh. A few agonizing seconds separated each blow, but Jesus bore the pain humbly without a single tear or harsh thought toward His tormentors. *He was oppressed and afflicted, yet He did not open His mouth; He was led like a lamb to the slaughter.* (Isaiah 53:7) Upon completion of the forty lashes, the soldiers again grabbed Jesus. They kicked and taunted Him along the walk back to Pilate. When they arrived at the Praetorium, more soldiers joined in and arranged a mock coronation.

THE CROWNING OF THORNS

They twisted some thorns into a crude crown and shoved it onto His head. *They put a purple robe on Him, then twisted together a crown of thorns and set it on Him. And they began to call out to Him, "Hail, King of the Jews!" Again and again they struck Him on the head with a staff and spit on Him.* (Mark 15:17–19) Striking Him, they continued to force the thorns farther into His head. These thorns were three inches long with needle-sharp points. They poked out well beyond the circle in all directions.

Jesus accepted every torture. He was determined to obey the will of His Father, even though every movement caused more pain. The soldiers continued to mock and beat Him, hitting Him on the head. The thorns pierced His scalp. Blood was now flowing from His head, face, back and shoulders with bruises all around His legs, already black from internal bleeding. Anyone would have collapsed by this time, but Jesus endured all of it without complaint.

The soldiers then pushed Jesus outside to Pilate, who was standing in front of a growing mob. Pilate mockingly asked, *"Shall I crucify your king?" The chief priests answered, "We have no king but Caesar."* (John 19:15) And there stood Jesus, *pierced for our transgressions, crushed for our iniquities.* (Isaiah 53:4) Ours were the sufferings he bore; ours are the sorrows He carried. But the mob shouted even louder, "Crucify Him." And there stood Jesus; *the punishment that brought us peace was upon Him, and by His wounds we are healed.* (Isaiah 53:5) Jesus was devastated by the continuing betrayal and weakened by the onslaught of blows. But he willingly received His cross, and they led Him out to crucify Him.

THE CARRYING OF THE CROSS

Christ's cross was large, heavy and rough. The wooden structure was made wide and thick. It was presumably made of local timber, still full of moisture and sap. Its tremendous weight was awkward and burdensome. We may also assume that its maker didn't smooth out the wood after he cut it. With the tools of the age, rough cut lumber had splinters comparable to small daggers. So as the soldiers dropped the massive cross onto Christ's shoulder, it added torment to torture, gouging Him ever deeper.

It was then time to begin the arduous walk up the trail of Calvary. At this point, Jesus was beaten and fatigued as not even the strongest of men could endure. His heroic strength stemmed from His powerful will and His unrelenting determination came from His love for us. As Jesus moved upward along the path, He found no encouragement to support His great trial. Instead He continued among more hitting, kicking, spitting and mocking from the people He loved. Jesus continued forward through this emotional duress and physical pain. In fact, His determination grew stronger upon each insult because He knew that His mercy was needed, now even more than just moments before. As more hatred was displayed by the people, more love emanated from Jesus, counteracting their wickedness with His goodness.

Jesus soon fell to the ground under the heavy cross. Sand stuck to His open wounds mixing with sweat and blood. Terrible itching and irritation now compounded intense pain. His hands were covered with blood, dirt, and wood splinters, rendering Him unable to care for Himself or even wipe His brow. Furthermore, this fall made the soldiers even more aggressive. Fearful that He might not be able to complete the journey, the soldiers forced a bystander to help Jesus carry the cross. Simon from Cyrene then proceeded to assist Jesus and the advancement continued. But Simon's assistance shortly went from handling a little weight to less and less. Soon he remained only to pacify the soldiers, thinking nothing of Christ's burden or purpose. Jesus fell a second time and then a third. The cross crashed down, crushing His body but not His will. He rose with more humility and walked on with greater desire.

THE CRUCIFIXION

They reached the destination where Christ was to be crucified, a place called "the skull." The soldiers took the cross from Jesus and laid it on the ground. Without hearing any last wish or statement from Jesus, they prepared Him for hanging.

They ripped off His garment and they nailed Him to the cross. Envision removing a bandage from a cut on your finger. Just the tape pulling away from the skin hurts, let alone the wound itself when stuck or dried to the bandage. Well, the entire skin of Christ's back was scraped off from the earlier scourging. The slashing was so severe that it gouged out chunks of His flesh. His shoulders were left with hardly any skin whatsoever. Now, hours later, His clothing had dried and stuck to His body. Did the soldiers have sympathy for Jesus? Did they carefully remove His garment? They aggressively ripped it from Him, reopening all of His wounds. Such pain is unimaginable and thus indescribable but to understand how much Jesus loves us, try to imagine that degree of suffering. He underwent that torture for each one of us.

Jesus was then thrown to the ground on His back. His body was shoved onto the cross and His arms and legs were stretched out by force. Then He caught sight of the fastening spikes. These splintered metal wedges were thick and crude. The soldiers drove the first spike through His wrist with a large mallet. A second was punched through His other hand, then one through His feet. Without the luxury of a quick death, Jesus endured to the last. He obeyed His Father's will and demonstrated His genuine love.

Each movement the soldiers made in raising the cross made another gouge in our Savior. Yet for love of us, Jesus endured the pain even longer as he hung on the cross in complete humility. In the midst of His anguish, there on the cross, He uttered His last words for mankind.

The first represents His infinite mercy. While looking out at those who tortured Him (who now mocked, beat and spit on Him) He said, *"Father, forgive them for they know not what they are doing."* (Luke 23:34) This means not only "Father, please don't hurt them," but "Father, please let them live with us in our home someday."

Christ's next words from the cross describe His unlimited love. In His final moment on earth, He still thought of us rather than Himself. He longs for us to discover His Truth, yearns for us to desire His Peace and thirsts for us to return His love. And so He said, *"I thirst."* (John 19:28) Jesus was not referring to any bodily need but to His infinite desire for the salvation of souls. He opened His sacred heart to us throughout His life and now in His death. *One of the soldiers pierced Jesus' side with a spear, bringing a sudden flow of blood and water.* (John 19:34) He demonstrated a virtuous life with His giving, teaching and healing. He made a death of unparalleled charity with His extraordinary suffering, heroic humiliation and supernatural atonement for our sins. Jesus did not yield to any limits and did not hesitate at any time. He sacrificed Himself completely that our lives may be complete in Him. *"I have told you this so that My joy may be in you and that your joy may be complete."* (John 15:11)

Jesus then cried out in a loud voice, *"Father, into your hands I commit my spirit." When He had said this, He breathed His last.* (Luke 23:46) Jesus Christ died that we may have life. He sacrificed the comfort of heaven to undergo pain and suffering so that we would know the extent of His love for us. He desires our appreciation for His effort and victory. If we do not think of Him in thanksgiving and avoid sin for Him, then we are like the people who killed Him. Do we dare flippantly think, What has God ever done for me? We should instead question ourselves: "What have I done for Him?" Jesus did not have to suffer to save us. He did it to exhibit His love for us that we may love Him in return. So let us be moved by appreciation and gratitude. Let us be moved to love our Savior. Let us love Him as He deserves to be loved.

15

APPRECIATING
THE SON OF GOD

With my dwindling faith in God, I had only a small appreciation for Jesus. I knew about His mission on earth. I knew that He died on a cross. But these generous favors never sank in deep. As I progressed in the business community, I regressed in my unity with God. What little appreciation I had for Christ was soon overshadowed by my desire for money and pleasure. I didn't know that a dormant faith soon fades away. I didn't know that an idle faith disappears altogether. I didn't know that we each have a duty to practice our faith in God, and nourish its growth by living His laws of love.

But no one in business would tell me that. They were only concerned about money and success. My business associates only cared about the prosperity I could give them. I was seduced by material wealth and I respected their greed while rejecting the treasure of God. And as I chased money it slowly blinded me until I could no longer see.

Without appreciation for Jesus, all that remained was a void in my soul, the desolation and emptiness of sin. But I wanted to find fulfillment again so how could I get back to God? What can bring us closer to Him?

JESUS OUR SAVIOR

Jesus has been aware of our existence since the beginning of time. He has loved each one of us from then until now and shall continue to love us forever. Christ's love is not idle but dynamic and overflowing as demonstrated by His extraordinary actions. It is through His life that we have been made and it is through His death that we have been saved. It is only because of His infinite merits that we become children of God and thereby inherit eternal life. *Yet to all who received Him, to those who believed in His name, He gave the right to become children of God — children born not of natural descent, nor of human decision or a husband's will, but born of God.* (John 1:12–13) No one could give us anything similar to these supernatural offerings of Jesus. Yet most of us don't fully appreciate His gifts. So let us now learn of His unlimited goodness so that we may more fully respond to His love.

Jesus accepted His Father's will and sacrificed Himself to atone for our sins. *"For God so loved the world that He gave His one and only Son, that whoever believes in Him shall not perish but have eternal life. For God did not send His Son into the world to condemn the world, but to save the world through Him."* (John 3:16–17) So for a period in time, Jesus left His heavenly state where He resided in perfect happiness. He humbled Himself for each of us by accepting a human body and dwelling in poverty as the lowest of men. *She wrapped Him in cloths and placed Him in a manger, because there was no room for them at the inn.* (Luke 2:7) Jesus loves us so much that He was willing to experience our mortal state while postponing His own glory. He not only sacrificed Himself at the end of His earthly life, but spent His whole life for our salvation, enduring hardship from the moment He was born. *"Get up," he said, "take the Child and His mother and escape to Egypt. Stay there until I tell you, for Herod is going to search for the Child to kill Him."* (Matthew 2:13)

Prior to His public ministry, Jesus spent thirty years with His earthly mother and father (Mary and Joseph). He did not concern Himself with pleasures but patiently waited for His mission. Daily routine becomes boring for us. And likewise, Christ's carpentry work must have been mundane and tedious, especially compared to heaven. Yet He patiently persisted due to His love of the Father's will and His concern for us. When the time drew near for Jesus to begin preaching, He went into the desert to fast and pray in preparation for His upcoming mission. There He underwent self-sacrifice and temptation for the benefit of our future salvation. *After fasting forty days and forty nights, He was hungry. The tempter came to Him and said, "If you are the Son of God, tell these stones to become bread." Jesus answered, "It is written: man does not live on bread alone, but on every word that comes from the mouth of God."* (Matthew 4:2–4)

Upon returning from the desert, Jesus began proclaiming the "Good News." *Whoever believes in the Son, has eternal life.* (John 3:36) And so Jesus started to teach. He walked and talked day and night, traveling down hot dusty roads. He experienced continual frustration from trying to teach love to people who didn't want to learn. *Coming to His hometown, He began teaching the people in their synagogue, and they were amazed. "Where did this Man get this wisdom and these miraculous powers?" they asked. "Isn't this the carpenter's Son? Isn't His mother's name Mary?" . . . "Where then did this Man get all these things?" And they took offense at Him.* (Matthew 13:54–57)

The religious leaders of the time also caused Him great sorrow. Regardless of His good example and teaching, they continued in their hypocrisy and sin. It was terribly disappointing for Jesus to discover that in spite of His effort of love, some people would never respond. And some would even rise up against Him. *The Pharisees went out and plotted how they might kill Jesus.* (Matthew 12:14) With full understanding of His Father's will, He accepted every sacrifice with the same love that He receives His humble friends. *"I praise You, Father, Lord of heaven and earth, because you have hidden these things from the wise and learned, and revealed them to little children."* (Matthew 11:25)

Filled with the determination of His Spirit, encouraged by trust in His Father, and moved by the power of love, Jesus continued His difficult work. He proceeded to teach the ignorant, heal the sick and feed the hungry through His compassionate heart. There are numerous accounts of His care and miraculous service to those in need. They all originate from His concern for the welfare of His brethren. *Great crowds came to Him, bringing the lame, the blind, the crippled, the mute, and many others, and laid them at His feet; and He healed them. . . . Jesus called His disciples to Him and said, "I have compassion for these people; they have already been with me three days and have nothing to eat. I do not want to send them away hungry, or they may collapse on the way."* (Matthew 15:30–32) That day Jesus performed the miracle of the loaves and fishes where He multiplied seven loaves of bread and a few small fish to feed over five thousand people. Jesus was also hungry but He helped His neighbors first before feeding Himself. *Love is patient, love is kind.* (1 Corinthians 13:4)

Another selfless act of Christ's great love is the unlimited blessings that He grants through the Holy Spirit. The Spirit Himself is a gift to us, imparted with boundless compassion. Jesus gives us His Holy Spirit to keep the Truth in us and refresh our virtue so that we can remain forever in love. *"I will ask the Father, and He will give you another Counselor to be with you forever — the Spirit of truth. The world cannot accept Him, because it neither sees Him nor knows Him. But you know Him, for He lives with you and will be in You."* (John 14:16–17)

Jesus knows that we cannot live a truly righteous life on our own. He also knows that we easily become distracted and confused, troubled and afraid, lonely and bored. Therefore, in His divine foresight and sympathy, He continues with us always through the indwelling presence of the Holy Spirit. *"I will not leave you as orphans; I will come to you. Before long, the world will not see Me anymore, but you will see Me. Because I live, you also will live. On that day you will realize that I am in the Father, and you are in Me, and I am in you."* (John 14:18–20) Let us then show our appreciation to Jesus by following His commands. We can then keep Him with us in companionship and peace, forever joined by His love. *"If anyone loves Me, he will obey my teaching. My Father will love him, and we will come to him and make our home with him."* (John 14:23)

Jesus also gives each person His own mother. There is no love comparable to motherly care. When Christ was on the cross, He saw before Him Mary His mother, and John, His disciple. He said to His mother, *"Dear woman, here is your Son,"* and to the Disciple, *"Here is your Mother."* (John 19:26) Theologians agree that Christ, when speaking to His disciple, was referring to each one of us. Those who turn toward heaven for help may receive it through their spiritual mother, the Blessed Virgin Mary. We may offer gifts to the Father, the Son, or the Holy Spirit through Mary. We may ask her to gain for us faith, hope and love or protection, perseverance and help. She is available to console us and ready to protect us with more energy and power than any natural mother. Our Immaculate Mother is a precious gift — for through her we receive all that is needed for this world, and through her we someday join God in the next.

Jesus gave His life for us in the most humiliating and painful way possible, demonstrating His enormous love for us while making it possible for us to be saved. During the time of Christ there was no lower humiliation than the punishment of crucifixion. There was no worse torment than suffering on the cross. And there has never existed any greater anguish than betrayal by one's own best friend. Yet Jesus underwent all of these miseries, all for the sake of us. Let us not demean this act by questioning why it was necessary. It was ordained by God for reasons beyond our understanding. Jesus loves us so much that He endured those events completely for our benefit. He did not accomplish this work of our salvation for any personal gain. He was already King of heaven and earth before He undertook this mission. But he sacrificed Himself in this staggering feat to demonstrate His love for us. His love is so extensive that He gives to us everything He has. His love for us is immeasurable. It is in fact, infinite. *"Greater love has no one but this, that He lay down His life for His friends."* (John 15:13) *For I am convinced that neither death nor life, neither angels nor demons, neither the present nor the future, nor any powers, neither height nor depth, nor anything else in all creation, will be able to separate us from the love of God that is in Christ Jesus our Lord.* (Romans 8:38–39)

16

GRATITUDE FOR
THE GIFT OF LIFE

After two years of working in the world I started my own business. Blessed with some talent and marketing skills I quickly obtained many clients. With work lining up and money rolling in, I became arrogant again. I purchased new clothes, new cars and a house and got caught in a web. I had large payments to support and a big ego, too, lurking like poisonous spiders. And where was God in my life? And where was His love that I once had? He was gone — not to be seen, for I shunned Him for worldly success. I replaced Him with money and fame.

Instead of being grateful to God, I began to act with indifference. Instead of searching for God's love, I desired my own satisfaction. I screamed at those who got in my way and would never admit my own errors. What had become of this once loving child? How could I have drifted so far? How would I become grateful again?

RESPONDING TO GOD'S LOVE

We are grateful when we acknowledge all that we have been given by responding to God's love. Then how do we properly respond? What debt do we owe? To what extent should we pay? How can we pay for the gift of our life? Can we repay Christ with a thousand or even a million dollars? How about paying him a billion dollars: is our life not worth more than money? The most precious thing we have is our life. The smallest quantity of life cannot be paid for by anything else, or all things combined. What then do we owe for our life but life itself? By accepting Christ's love with our hearts and recognizing His gifts with our minds, we can overcome our selfishness. We become free from self-centered interests, and open to thank Jesus by giving Him our life. And it is precisely this gift that enables our salvation. *"For whoever wants to save his life will lose it, but whoever loses his life for Me will find it."* (Matthew 16:25)

So how much of our life is a just contribution? *"What can a man give in exchange for his soul?"* (Matthew 16:26) How about one hour each day? Currently most Christians give a few hours a week for Sunday Mass or church service so an additional hour per day appears to be ample. Thus if we gave twelve hours each day that would be a gigantic amount, and surely must be more than fair? But is it? Christ gave us our whole life and saved our whole soul. So is giving Him back one half of our life just? Is that how much our life is worth:

half of a life? No, our life is worth a full life, and our soul is worth a full soul. So it is only just that we give Jesus our entire life. We can then act unselfishly and provide for the poor rather than buying needless luxuries for ourselves. *"For what good will it be for a man if he gains the whole world, yet forfeits his soul?"* (Matthew 16:26)

But let us not be overwhelmed or discouraged by this news because with every part we give Christ, He gives us much more in return. *"No one who has left home or brothers or sisters or mother or father or children or fields for Me and the Gospel will fail to receive a hundred times as much in this present age, and in the age to come, eternal life."* (Mark 10:29–30) The logic of the world confuses us and leads us away from realizing the supernatural power of love. **With God's love, the more sacrifice we make, the more joy we take.**

Whenever we act with love, we uncover a peaceful reward that we never initially expected. This mystery is most apparent in assisting children. Let us recall the times in our lives when we were asked to give a child a bath or take them to the movies, and we reluctantly did so only to help. And during the event we happened to glance at the funny little creature and without any particular reason we just started to laugh. We suddenly acknowledged love in the child, and if we were really selfless in helping, we soon forgot the reasons for our earlier hesitation and began to enjoy the experience. We usually learn something in the process of giving, and afterward we notice that we have just gained more than we had given. *Give to the Most High as He has given to you; give generously to the Lord according to what you have; the Lord will repay, He will reward you sevenfold.* (Sirach 35:9–11)

We likewise receive great benefits from our prayers, sacrifices and adorations to God. We sometimes behave as if we are making an enormous sacrifice to pray. This fallacy occurs when we struggle before church service, pondering the activities we are giving up as if we are exerting this great effort for God. When we renounce this selfish thinking we realize the peace and comfort we receive at church. **We then understand that it is not we who favor God but He Who satisfies us.** *My soul finds rest in God alone; my salvation comes from Him.* (Psalm 62:1)

Think about a cigarette smoker with a serious heart condition: a person who has recently been told by his doctor that unless he stops smoking now, he will die very soon. He might begrudgingly quit, complaining about the doctor and the great sacrifice he is making. But he soon discovers that his chest pains are gone and his harsh cough has disappeared. Then he realizes that by changing his ways he has not forfeited his freedom but gained a better life. *"It is not the healthy who need a doctor, but the sick. I have not come to call the righteous, but sinners to repentance."* (Luke 5:31)

The world would have us believe that freedom consists in abandoning laws. Most of us have been taught that rules constrict liberty thus hindering our enjoyment of life. But the only time we are truly restricted is when we are slaves to sin. For example, when addicted to any substance, we are compelled by our bodily craving to seek it out, obtain it and use it. This vice can be something that we know to be unhealthy and deep down we prefer to avoid the activity, but we participate in it anyway. It costs money, time, and effort and sometimes it takes even more from us (relationships and love and life). Yet we go through this ridiculous procedure despite our better conscience against it. Now that is a description of slavery — the slaves we become to sin. But true independence exists in a relationship with Jesus where we follow His commands. He leads us to love and happiness by setting our free will free. *"Then you will know the truth, and the truth will set you free." They answered Him, "We are Abraham's descendants and have never been slaves of anyone. How can you say that we shall be set free?" Jesus replied, "I tell you the truth, everyone who sins is a slave to sin. Now a slave has no permanent place in the family, but a son belongs to it forever."* (John 8:32–35)

Let us then show our gratitude to Jesus by following His commands. We will not be disappointed with any loss of liberty, rather filled with joy in our newly-found friend. **For when we truly love someone, our actions of love become effortless.** And the more we come to know Him, the more we grow to love Him, making it easier to obey His commands. *The man who says, "I know Him," but does not do what He commands is a liar, and the truth is not in him. But if anyone obeys His word, God's love is truly made complete in him. This* *is how we know we are in Him: whoever claims to live in Him must walk as Jesus did.* (1 John 2:3–6) Let us not be afraid of this challenge because Jesus assures us, *"Everything is possible for him who believes."* (Mark 9:23) So let us not run away in fear but walk close by our Savior with faith and hope. Let us take courage from His love and know that the farther we walk, the easier the road becomes. And when we are distracted or tired, Love's energy will carry us along.

One night a man dreamed that he was walking along the beach with the Lord. Across the sky flashed scenes from his life. For each scene he noticed two sets of footprints in the sand; one belonged to him, and the other to the Lord. When the last scene of his life flashed before him, he looked back at the footprints in the sand. He noticed that many times along the path of his life there was only one set of footprints. He also noticed that it happened at the very lowest and saddest times of his life. This really bothered him and he questioned the Lord about it. "Lord, You said that once I decided to follow You, You would walk with me all the way. But I have noticed that at the most troublesome times in my life, there is only one set of footprints. I don't understand why, when I needed You most You would leave me." The Lord replied, "My precious child, I love you and I would never leave you. During your times of trial and suffering, when you see only one set of footprints; it was then that I carried you." ["Footprints," author unknown]

Our gratitude can shape the way we live, so that we may love Jesus and follow Him into heaven. *"I am the Way and the Truth and the Life. No one comes to the Father except through Me."* (John 14:6) Obedience to the teachings of Christ not only ensures eternal life but gives us a much happier life on earth. Happiness is already present within us. We simply need to remove our attention away from disruptive worldly desires and focus on the great peace that resides within. *"The kingdom of God does not come with your careful observation, nor will people say, 'Here it is,' or, 'There it is,' because the kingdom of God is within you."* (Luke 17:20–21)

To find the joyful comfort of paradise, we need to show gratitude for the love and beauty of God that exists inside ourselves. When we begin to accept this treasure within us, our behavior adjusts accordingly. **Instead of feeling anxious by trying to get what we want, we remain happy with what we have.** *"Do not store up for yourselves treasures on earth, where moth and rust destroy, and where thieves break in and steal. But store up for yourselves treasures in heaven, where moth and rust do not destroy, and where thieves do not break in and steal. For where your treasure is, there your heart will be also."* (Matthew 6:19–21)

This simple satisfaction is a tremendous step along our journey toward the goal of love. With our positive response of appreciating God, we find our true peace in Him. When we discover the perfect happiness found only in God, we receive the incentive needed to minimize the distractions of the world outside. We can then center ourselves on the main attraction inside. *For everything in the world — the cravings of sinful man, the lust of his eyes and the boasting of what he has and does — comes not from the Father but from the world. The world and its desires pass away, but the man who does the will of God lives forever.* (1 John 2:16–17) There is nothing wrong with participating in the ordinary events of the world, but they will give us no lasting happiness unless they involve our love. **For regarding our joy on this earth and beyond, the only essential element is the maturity of God's love within us.** *"You are worried and upset about many things, but only one thing is needed."* (Luke 10:41–42)

DEVELOPING HAPPINESS

17

THE BENEFITS OF PRAYER

After three years of owning a business I continued to buy everything in sight, including people and pleasure. But I never was truly happy. Deep down I was lonely and worried. I had two stomach ulcers by the age of twenty-eight, and lungs damaged by cigarettes. Then everything in the world that I fashioned began to pull apart at the seams. My creation crashed down around me to make way for the creation of God. As I began to lose money and friends I became aware of my abuse of God's goodness. Amidst devastating failures and depression my only recourse was prayer. I thank God that my instinctive reaction was to run back to Him. With shame as my ally and humility my friend I came back to God in prayer, begging for His forgiveness.

God did forgive me and He helped me rebuild most of what had collapsed. He returned my possessions and found me new friends, all through His response to my prayers. He healed me inside and out through Christ, soon restoring everything that was lost. So I never understand why we don't pray more to the God Who is our All. We're simply asking our Father to help us, or thanking Him for His love. Maybe we don't yet realize the great benefits of prayer.

RECEIVING GOD THROUGH PRAYER

In order for us to receive Jesus we need to invite Him in. This opening of our hearts in humility begins with prayer: a request of God to help us to know Him that we may learn to love Him. *"Ask and it will be given to you, seek and you shall find, knock and the door will be opened to you."* (Matthew 7:7) The strength of our prayer comes from a sincere desire to be with God. At first, it does not matter what motivates our desire. A person may be extremely lonely and therefore want God for company. Another person might be in pain and seeking God for comfort, while yet another could be looking for Him to get out of trouble. The particular reason for wanting God should be of no concern in the beginning. The important matter is that we have a desire for Him. When we first start searching for God, our motivations will always be selfish because His grace has not yet grown in us. As we continue to pray, love grows in us. Then our selfishness decreases and we start making small acts of love. As God's tree of love grows and branches in us, our motivations convert to loving intentions. *"The kingdom of heaven is like a mustard seed, which a man took and planted in his field. Though it is the smallest of all your seeds, yet when it grows, it is the largest of garden plants and becomes a tree, so that the birds of the air come and perch in its branches."* (Matthew 13:31)

To establish a desire for God or to increase our existing fondness of Him, let us remember that everything comes from Him; including desire itself. Praying to increase our hunger for God is the most effective way of receiving it. *"For everyone who asks receives; he who seeks finds; and to him who knocks, the door will be opened."* (Matthew 7:8) Even if we don't yet know God, we can just open our heart to Him. Jesus recommends starting alone in a quiet surrounding. *"When you pray, go into your room, close the door and pray to your Father, Who is unseen. Then your Father, Who sees what is done in secret, will reward you."* (Matthew 6:6) We can then say to Him, "God, I have no idea what I'm doing. I have no idea if You even exist, but please God — please let me know. Please don't leave me here all alone feeling estranged and awkward. Please come into my life. I'm willing to take a chance on You. I'm willing to try to know You. I want to know You. I need to know You. I have to know You. I want to be happy. . . . I want to love. . . . I want to live!"

We should also know that prayer requires persistence. We should not give up after only a few sittings or only a few days. God is present and He hears us. He may respond quickly but usually He waits. *"Suppose one of you has a friend, and he goes to him at midnight and says, 'Friend, lend me three loaves of bread, because a friend of mine on a journey has come to me and I have nothing to set before him.' Then the one inside answers, 'Don't bother me. The door is already locked, and my children are with me in bed. I can't get up and give you anything.' I tell you, though he will not get up and give him the bread because he is his friend, yet because of the man's persistence he will get up and give him as much as he needs."* (Luke 11:5)

God rewards our prayers according to our effort and trust, which is displayed by our persistence. The more we pray and the longer we wait for God's response, the greater our reward becomes. Saint Monica fervently prayed for fifteen years for the conversion of her son, Augustine. She asked God first that her son would stop his womanizing ways. She asked God second that her son would be baptized. And thirdly, she asked God to help her son stop teaching heresy.

After fifteen long years, God answered all of her prayers — proportionate to her persistence. First, Augustine not only stopped womanizing, he made a vow of celibacy for the glory of God. Secondly, Augustine was not only baptized, he became a priest and later a bishop. Thirdly, Augustine not only discontinued teaching heresy, he became the Church's greatest defender against it. Augustine has since been canonized a saint and is honored as one of the few "doctors" of the Catholic Church. God rewarded Saint Monica's effort and trust in a way that far exceeded her highest expectations.

Salvation on our own is impossible but with God all things are possible. That is why we surrender ourselves to God in prayer. We humbly ask Him to help us by fulfilling His love in us, so we can be happy with Him. We need to understand that difficulties in life are allowed by God to bring us back to Him. For most of us it is only problems or difficulties that generate our desire for God. We want Him to rescue us from the loneliness, the pain, or the trouble we encounter. Many people who have great wealth do not feel a need for God, and therefore don't take the time to know Him. But those lucky people who suffer in this world have incentive to search for Him, and through prayer may find Him. Thus we should not let our motives distract us but instead let our desire for God increase in any way possible. Then with time, He will purify our motivation, making it more fitting of His goodness and beauty. *"With man this is impossible, but not with God; all things are possible with God."* (Mark 10:27)

Why let problems get in the way of happiness with God? Why let laziness get in the way? Why let desires for pleasure hinder our growth of love? Why let daily worries interrupt the great peace of God? Why not believe that such joy is possible? **God exists here and now!** He is available to us right now. God wants all of us to unite with Him. *"Your Father in heaven is not willing that any of these little ones should be lost."* (Matthew 18:14) He wants us all to be happy now and forever more. God wants to give us Himself! All we need is to want Him, then we can ask to receive Him. *"Which of you fathers, if your son asks for a fish, will give him a snake instead? Or if he asks for an egg, will give him a scorpion? If you then, though you are evil, know how to give good gifts to your children, how much more will your Father in heaven give the Holy Spirit to those who ask Him!"* (Luke 11:11)

So let us have confidence in the promises of God

and discover the power of prayer. Anything we ask for (consistent with God's will for us) shall be given to us through Christ. *"I will do whatever you ask in my name, so that the Son may bring glory to the Father. You may ask Me for anything in my name, and I will do it."* (John 14:13–14) Confidence in God comes from His love for us and develops with our belief and trust. Thus our faith and hope beget the charity that assures all answers to our requests. *"If you have faith as small as a mustard seed, you can say to this mountain, 'Move from here to there,' and it will move. Nothing will be impossible for you."* (Matthew 17:21) This true love that generates real happiness is the same supernatural energy that satisfies our every desire. The love of God has no limit but is only brought forth through our faith in Him. *"Whatever you ask for in prayer, believe that you have received it, and it will be yours."* (Mark 11:24) We can start asking God for this faith right now. The great power of love that yields abounding joy is available to us this instant. And we can obtain this everlasting love by accepting Christ's offer: *"My Father will give you whatever you ask in My name. Until now you have not asked for anything in My name. Ask and you will receive, and your joy will be complete."* (John 16:24)

18

THE NEED FOR REPENTANCE

Off I went again with all of God's gifts and blessings. But a few years later I fell back into the same
trap. I was too busy with work to continue in prayer.
I was now working in two locations. I purchased of-
fices, homes and cars in my home town and overseas. I
slipped in my prayer life and stopped going to church
all together. What a fool I was. Knowing that God
gave me everything and knowing that He deserves my
love, I tossed Him aside once again accepting money
and pleasure instead. I sold out to the world again,
seduced by fortune and fame. It was purely accidental
— I wouldn't purposely sell my soul. But little by little that is exactly what happened to me. I slowly but
surely spent less time with God and more time with
self-gratification.

Then God in His mercy responded again, only this
time in a powerful fury. The life style I created came
crashing down with nothing left standing. I was left
confused, battered and bruised with only one possible recourse — prayer to our one, true God. So back
to God I went on my knees, begging forgiveness and
love. God heard me but remained silent, testing my

resolve. I continued to pray each day. Again and again I went before God, asking Him to forgive me. More than six months passed without any reply but I kept going back to pray.

Then near despair but without giving up on God, I admitted my own unworthiness. And in hopelessness of self I gave all to God and trusted Him beyond everything. I promised Him that I was finished with selfishness and that I never would go back again, but live all future years only for Him. After several months of this determined resolution I received my answer from God. I understand now that He was waiting for a true repentance, a deep sorrow for my sins with a strong desire to change.

ACCEPTING GOD THROUGH PERSONAL CHANGE

Repentance begins the opening of our hearts and allows our reception of God's love. *And so John came, baptizing in the desert region and preaching a baptism of repentance for the forgiveness of sins.* (Mark 1:4) Repentance is a deep sorrow for sin with a conviction to change. It requires a firm commitment to begin a new life. When we live in the state of sin we block our awareness of God's grace. *The light shines in the darkness, but the darkness has not understood it.* (John 1:4–5) But when we acknowledge our error and ask God for His companionship and commit to obey His commands, He forgives our sins and welcomes us back into His grace. *"Whoever has My commands and obeys them, he is the one who loves Me. He who loves Me will be loved by My Father, and I too will love him and show Myself to him."* (John 14:21) We begin to recognize God's presence and receive the joy of His love. When repentance opens our hearts we befriend God. **With God we inherit love and with love we receive the true peace that delivers perfect happiness.**

"There was a man who had two sons. The younger one said to his father, 'Father, give me my share of the estate.' So he divided his property between them. Not long after that, the younger son got together all he had, set off for a distant country and there squandered his wealth in wild living. After he had spent everything, there was a severe famine in that whole country, and he began to be in need. So he went and hired himself out to a citizen of

that country, who sent him to his fields to feed pigs. He longed to fill his stomach with the pods that the pigs were eating, but no one gave him anything. When he came to his senses, he said, 'How many of my father's hired men have food to spare, and here I am starving to death! I will set out and go back to my father and say to him: Father, I have sinned against heaven and against you. I am no longer worthy to be called your son; make me like one of your hired men.' So he got up and went to his father. But while he was still a long way off, his father saw him and was filled with compassion for him; he ran to his son, threw his arms around him and kissed him. The son said to him, 'Father, I have sinned against heaven and against you. I am no longer worthy to be called your son.' But the father said to his servants, 'Quick! Bring the best robe and put it on him. Put a ring on his finger and sandals on his feet. Bring the fattened calf and kill it. Let's have a feast and celebrate. For this son of mine was dead and is alive again; he was lost and is found.' So they began to celebrate." (Luke 15:11–24)

There is a great benefit in repentance — the gain of true happiness now and forever. But the effort should not be lightly considered — for it is a difficult task. It is easier to act wrongly out of pride and selfishness than to act rightly from humility and love. Developing the willpower to live honorably is difficult. We need to recondition ourselves from bad habits, generated from the bad example of the world and our own self-centeredness. To understand our need to eliminate bad habits, let us consider the following example.

We are late driving back from work and anxious to get home to watch a championship game. Suddenly a car pulls out in front of us, causing us to swerve and nearly hit oncoming traffic. Enraged with anger do we honk our horn several times (even though it is far too late for any warning sound)? Do we yell obscenities at the other driver while shaking a closed fist at him? Do we try passing by in rage trying to get the driver's attention? Or do we simply become angry at the other driver and then complain about the incident to the first person we see?

Even though the above reactions seem to be acceptable behavior, they are not. None of them are actions of love but actions of anger, pride and contempt. Regardless of the intention of the other driver (who most probably made a simple mistake) there is no benefit from any of the above reactions. But we are conditioned to give any disturbing action at least an equally disturbing reaction, regardless of whether it is right to do so. This incorrect training forms very bad habits. They become deeply rooted in pride, which continues to grow in us to our own detriment. All of the above reactions are based on self-centeredness which ultimately comes from pride. How dare that person cut in front of me! Who does he think he is? He's certainly no better than me! . . . or . . . How dare that person, I'm the one in a hurry here! If I don't get home fast I'll. . ., I could have . . . My car almost . . . I, I, I, My, My, My, Me, Me, Me . . . it is all pride.

We need to be reconditioned to act from the humil-

WHAT'S LOVE GOT TO DO WITH IT?

ity of love rather than the pride of evil. This is a difficult process because instead of our automatic reactions of aggression, we need to choose a more loving reaction governed by patience, understanding and forgiveness. Repentance empowers this new direction by establishing the desire to act from good rather than from evil. It transforms us to respond with loving concern rather than with thoughts of our own misfortune. A loving person would respond to the driving episode with an inquisitive wonder instead of a vengeful outburst. The truly loving person, before considering his own circumstances, would first speak from patience, "Wow, that driver must be in an awful hurry." He might then comment from understanding, "What a poor driver, he must be just starting out behind the wheel." He can then forgive, "It's okay, sometimes we have to learn from our mistakes." Initially, we need understanding to forgive but after some time practicing, God provides us with more love which enables forgiveness regardless of understanding. This gift eliminates anger and frustration and maintains our continuous peace.

Let us then turn to God in humility. Let us approach Him with an open heart to ask for His compassion and help. We can sometimes be hindered by shame or guilt but let us remember the power of love. God never separates Himself from us. It is only we who choose sin, then toil in the trap of our own remorse. We need to bring ourselves before Christ and be open to accept His forgiveness. *They made her stand before the group and said to Jesus, "Teacher, this woman*

THE NEED FOR REPENTANCE

was caught in the act of adultery. In the Law Moses com-manded us to stone such women. Now what do You say?"
... "If any one of you is without sin, let him be the first to throw a stone at her." ... At this, those who heard began to go away one at a time, the older ones first, until only Jesus was left, with the woman still standing there. Jesus straightened up and asked her, "Woman, where are they? Has no one condemned you?" "No one, Sir," she said. "Then neither do I condemn you," Jesus declared, "Go now and leave your life of sin." (John 8:3–11)

If a friend gives out information that we had asked to remain secret, his behavior will certainly offend us. It would trouble our relationship and we would not want to speak to him. But if the next day he comes to our home having realized his mistake, how can we turn him away? With even a little love, we would respond with forgiveness and care. And if we had deeper love we would welcome our friend back with joy. So let us not be afraid to go to our friend Jesus and ask for His pardon and peace. Let us run to our Savior with warm appreciation, confident in His mercy and love. **And to enjoy this great love let us open our hearts by first opening our minds to repentance.**

"Suppose one of you has a hundred sheep and loses one of them. Does he not leave the ninety-nine in the open country and go after the lost sheep until he finds it? And when he finds it, he joyfully puts it on his shoulders and goes home. Then he calls his friends and neighbors together and says, 'Rejoice with me; I have found my lost sheep.' I tell you that in the same way there is more rejoicing in

heaven over one sinner who repents than over ninety-nine righteous persons who do not need to repent." "Or suppose a woman has ten silver coins and loses one. Does she not light a lamp, sweep the house and search carefully until she finds it? And when she finds it, she calls her friends and neighbors together and says, 'Rejoice with me; I have found my lost coin.' In the same way, I tell you, there is rejoicing in the presence of the angels of God over one sinner who repents." (Luke 15:4–10)

19

THE EMBRACE OF LOVE

I was thirty-three years old when God answered my prayer. I wanted a life of His goodness and truth to replace the evil and lies. I was trained by experts of commerce — the new breed of the American dream. I was one of the young professionals who are taught to seek wealth and pleasure and led to believe they will find happiness there. The great American lie, misleading many people. Following those ways, I received emptiness, pain and desolation again and again. There is no love in money and it limits our joy, making it temporary and shallow. God knew that deep down I was searching for Him and that I was continually confused by my surroundings. So on that great day He answered my prayers and sent His Son Jesus to help me.

I had just received some devastating news about yet another life crisis. This was by far the worst, and it was obvious that no solution existed. It was the thirtieth crushing situation in a year of continuous blows. But this one destroyed any chance of recovery and I knew I was totally helpless. So again I went back to God, as I did so many times before, hoping beyond hope for His help. I was completely ruined and extinguished outside and inside fully spent. I had not the energy to get up and walk and no will to live any longer. So I gave my life to God by giving my will to Him, saying never again will I move without You, not even to eat or breathe. I said, "If You want me, here I am — otherwise let me die here in grief — wipe my name away from existence." Just then at the depth of my anguish, something incredible happened: the light of the Lord, our God.

A mist of Love descended upon me passing all the way through. The mist on my right flowed through to my left while the mist on my left flowed through to my right. The peaceful sensation above me flowed down through me right to the floor, and all around me was Love. An aura of great peace surrounded me, flowing in me and through me all at once. Jesus Himself had penetrated my being and remained to embrace my soul. My body was captivated while my five senses were suspended and still. I could not move, see, taste, or smell, nor did I even want to. But my interior was gripped in pure joy, seeing the beauty of God. I was hearing the sound of His love, tasting the flavor of His peace, smelling the scent of His kindness and feeling the warmth of His care. I was completely engulfed in the embrace of Jesus, overwhelmed by His majesty yet uplifted in His love. Whatever the time, it seemed an eternity of bliss contained in a matter of minutes. The world may have seen ten minutes go by but to me it was a lifetime of happiness. The comfort and joy and peace of God's Love was far beyond what I can describe. But to communicate the glory that awaits us in heaven, I tell you this to give you hope: I would gladly exchange a lifetime of worldly pleasure for just ten minutes of that Love. So believe me that God's love brings us happiness and that we can have heaven on earth. Never mind the effort and sacrifice because God makes everything worthwhile. He dwells in our hearts while establishing in us the peace and joy of His love. *"The kingdom of God is within you."* (Luke 17:21)

ENJOYING GOD THROUGH LOVE

In God's will there is a definite plan and God's plan for us is to engage in a relationship with Him. He invites us to be His friends and to live with Him forever. God dwells in perfect love for *God is love.* (1 John 4:16) We therefore need His love so that we may live forever with Him in harmony. **Life's purpose is a journey of love by which we can someday (through practice and prayer) arrive at the state of perfect love.** We can then receive the prize of love: perfect happiness with each other and God, together in heaven.

Many people think that love is a physical attraction which offers a pleasurable feeling. But this is not true love because true love is completely unselfish. All real love comes from God, and He gives us a progressively deeper comprehension as we travel along our spiritual journey. Our understanding of love at five years of age is different than when we are twenty-five and yet again different at fifty. Our awareness and understanding of love develops in us through our education, experience and the grace of God. The theological definition of love is the only true definition because love is a theological virtue.

True love is the unselfish desire for another persons' benefit and the action it imposes. Thus, love is as love does. We can easily desire someone's benefit, but true love isn't demonstrated until we make an actual effort, especially an unselfish effort. *Dear children, let us not love with words or tongue but with actions and* *in truth.* (1 John 3:18) So on our journey of love, if this is the start, where do we finish? We know that ultimately we are to be with God, Who exists in a state of perfect love. We therefore need to grow into perfect love ourselves. What then is perfect love?

Perfect love is the unselfish desire for complete union with the beloved. Perfect love begets the lover's active pursuit of transformation into complete union with the beloved. This does not suggest any loss of identity, rather unified identity. For example, a blossom's colorful petals are all separate identities yet each interacts with the others forming the organic union that is a flower. The soul or spirit of every being encompasses its own will, and each has formed its own idea of what is good for itself. But we, being imperfect by nature, cannot know each particular good for ourselves and therefore cannot will our own best good. But God, Who is perfect by nature, always knows our every good. And God, because of His true love, always wills our highest good. God knows that our highest good is perfect love, which we can have only in Him because He is the source of it. God therefore knows that our highest good is oneness with Him, which is the only true manifestation of this perfect love.

Each colorful petal is joined together with the others to form the flower, and remains an individual part while sharing a common purpose. Each unique person joins together with God, and maintains an individual identity while sharing a common purpose. The petals' common purpose is the display of beauty which establishes their goodness. Our common purpose is the display of goodness which establishes our beauty. Sharing a common purpose with God means conforming our wills to His. Because God's will is perfect and our wills are not, it is up to us to change, conforming our will to His. When we desire God and are open to change to be like Him, we enable ourselves to exist with Him in perfect love. **The height of our spiritual growth is to lovingly surrender to the will of God to reach the goal of our life's journey: to dwell together with Him.**

A normal first reaction to conforming our will to God's will is great hesitation with apprehensions of boredom and stagnation. But these anxious thoughts are completely opposite from the truth. The reality is that life with God is uplifting, dynamic and peaceful. To encounter God in this lifetime we need the steady elimination of our selfishness and the resulting growth of our love. The fuel required for this adventure of spiritual growth is belief in God's existence, trust in God's promises and love of God's goodness; otherwise known as faith, hope and charity. These three qualities are called the theological virtues because they come from God.

Spiritual growth is a divine endeavor and thus requires divine help. To prepare ourselves to receive this help, we must empty our minds of all that is not God while opening our hearts to receive all that is. This preparation of our soul begins with spiritual knowledge coupled with our desire to grow. To desire something, we need to know first what that something is.

To desire spiritual growth is to want to conform our will to God's will. So what is God's will that we may desire it and learn to love it?

God's will is given to us through the gospel message of Jesus. It starts with God's primary objective in creating us. God desires us to be with Him now and forever. *"Father, I want those You have given Me to be with Me where I am [heaven]."* (John 17:24) The next desire of God is for us to follow His commandments that we may live in peace and accept His promise of eternal joy. Jesus summarized the commandments to make them simple for us. *"'Love the Lord your God with all your heart and with all your soul and with all your mind.' This is the first and greatest commandment. And the second is like it: 'Love your neighbor as yourself.' All the Law and the Prophets hang on these two commandments."* (Matthew 22:37–40) Both of these divine instructions profoundly start with love. **God's will for us is obvious: that we engage in love.** This brings us back to the purpose of life, the spiritual journey of love. We need to learn loving behavior so we can live in peace and discover real happiness, conforming to God's will while attaining heaven.

Anyone who has even moderately tasted the abundant sweetness of true love would agree that it is not dull. They likewise couldn't describe it as stagnant or boring. True love brings with it a mystical blend of enjoyable experience. True love is exciting yet tranquil, dynamic yet contented, ever changing yet permanent. True love is the most wonderful gift we could ever receive and yet it is just a prelude to God's invitation. The perfect love that God desires for us can not be described in words, but only communicated through personal experience. God sometimes grants us a hint of heaven by allowing us a taste of perfect love. What incredible joy we find there with overwhelming peace. **Awestruck with God's presence, captivated in delight, we become motionless in the enchantment of love.**

God has prepared great delights for us, accessible through the virtue of love. This news of Jesus is certainly *Good News* and it gets even better. God allows us to experience the happiness of true love with each other anytime we wish. And sometimes He allows us to experience the immense joy of His perfect love, without having to wait for heaven. God sometimes rewards us with spiritual experiences of deep peace. *"The peace of God, that surpasses all understanding."* (Philippians 4:7)

These unique divine touches are pure graces from God, completely unmerited by ourselves, but given to us as an enticement to more eagerly pursue love in this world. God's gift of spiritual consolations is reserved within His perfect judgment. However, we can prepare ourselves to receive them more frequently. As we constantly work toward improving ourselves by practicing virtue and avoiding vice, we steadily progress in eliminating selfishness and growing in love. The more we practice love for God, the more we grow in love from God. The more we grow in love, the more we do God's will, thus the more open we become to receive God's assistance. This help that God readily gives us comes through many spiritual graces — some of which are joyful encounters within His loving embrace.

So how do we grow in love? It is very general to say, "Practice virtue and avoid vice." So what can we specifically do? How do we prepare ourselves to receive God's grace? The answer to these questions is one and the same and starts with the conditions necessary for love. Love is where God is and God is where love is. If we want love to exist in us we need to receive God in us. **This is the one and only condition necessary to obtain love, that we obtain God.** *". . . that they may be one as We are one: I in them and You in Me. May they be brought to complete unity to let the world know that You sent Me and have loved them even as You have loved Me."* (John 17:22)

So if love is God's desire and He is available to join us now — why aren't we currently filled with His love? Simply because we are currently filled up to capacity with everything else. We house all kinds of non-Godly things which block the entrance of God, thus blocking the entrance of love. We are each an earthen vessel, once completely open to God's perfect love. But throughout our life we have hardened the surface by our disobedience to God's Holy Will.

Our selfishness has allowed worldly desires to overtake an area of our soul previously occupied by love. The desire for self-gratification grows like a spiritual cancer in us, filling a major share of the limited space available. Compounded with vanity and vice, evil can surround our will and smother our great fire of love.

The resulting embers are pushed down in our soul where they remain somewhat hidden, and difficult to summon except by renewed love of God. Without God's true love we lack His true happiness, and are instead overcome with worry and anxiety. **To rediscover the joy of our youth we must now reclaim our most beautiful domain and prepare for the presence of God again.**

Much of our previous attention has been scattered on problems and bad habits which now require our diligent retraining. These worldly trappings are numerous and include the following obstacles.

Residual anger, frustration or anxiety which have been developed from previous relationships — whatever we haven't completely forgiven is currently obstructing God's holy presence and blocking our ability to love.

Also inhibiting God's cooperation are bad habits and ill-formed tendencies (profanity, anger, manipulation of others or over-indulgent use of food, alcohol, tobacco or television). We can easily become weighed down with these activities and habits.

Further inhibiting God's perfect love is our pride. Self-centered, judgmental, demanding, or rude behavior are all signs of pride, which is truly the root of all vice. We need to be purified of this sinful condition so that we can be open to love.

Additional barriers to our happiness include unnecessary expectations and desires (our incessant craving for materials and pleasures). There is nothing intrinsically wrong with cars, boats or toys and nothing wrong with harmless activities. However, so many of us live so fully immersed in materialism that any visiting alien would think that people are made for toys rather than toys for people. Many of us maintain hedonistic attitudes and make sensual pleasures our primary goal.

Unfortunately we are all encumbered by these obstacles to grace, each of us to varying degrees. Christ's good news is that with His help we can overcome these hindrances. With faith in God we should be optimistic because He is already present within us, even if just as an ember now. And with hope in God we can be confident because He only needs a tiny spark to ignite a blazing fire. Let us never be discouraged because we maintain a most precious gift from God — our free will. When we use our will to want God, and we exert the effort to attain Him, we start to behave in harmony with His intention. We begin to adhere to God's will, inviting Him to enter our being. He will then come to dwell within us, bringing His perfect love to establish in us a wonderful peace which begets our true happiness.

20

THE FRUITS OF TRUST

Several years have passed since my deeply felt experience of Love. Jesus communicated many things to me then, now permanently affixed to my heart. He left me changed forever and gave me a constant appreciation of His goodness. But He left me uncured of my dysfunctional will power and bodily addictions as well. I had to start a course of recovery, reconditioning myself along the way. Alone this would have been impossible, but I remembered the power of prayer. So with repentance, trust, and prayer I lived one day at a time and slowly climbed back into life, this time the real life which is Love.

I diligently worked to untangle my problems and have recently completed that task. I am now happily married with four children. We are growing more in love with God and thank Him for every moment we share. God maintains our love, peace and happiness enabling some growth each day. We remain open to God, always accepting His Will and His Way. He keeps His Light shining in us through our window of faith and hope. And we keep the glass clean through humility and trust. Everything good comes from God and for

His children He always chooses the best. So we trust our Creator by obeying His commands and following His every desire. And ever since that day of years past I am always happy and fair, because since I learned my lesson I forever trust in God's care.

ATTAINING GOD THROUGH TRUST

How do we make the effort to attain true happiness in God? We first decide to desire God and therefore to desire love. We can then proceed according to the following laws of love: *"'Love the Lord your God with all your heart and all your soul and with all your mind.' . . . And . . . 'Love your neighbor as yourself.'"* (Matthew 22:37–39)

In order to fulfill these commands we need to practice them in trust, then spiritually grow in love by steady progression. We advance in peace by maturing in love, step by step along the following path:

ADHERENCE TO THE TEN COMMANDMENTS
(Exodus 20:1–17)

1. I am the Lord your God, you shall not worship any gods before Me.

2. You shall not misuse the name of the Lord.

3. Remember to keep holy the Sabbath day.

4. Honor your father and mother.

5. You shall not murder.

6. You shall not commit adultery.

7. You shall not steal.

8. You shall not give false witness.

9. You shall not covet your neighbor's goods.

10. You shall not covet your neighbor's wife.

AVOIDANCE OF THE SEVEN CAPITAL (DEADLY) SINS

Pride — the unjustified high opinion of oneself, vanity

Wrath — excessive anger, rage, fury

Greed — excessive desire of money or material objects

Gluttony — the overindulgence of food or pleasures

Lust — excessive appetite for sensual pleasure

Envy — inordinate desire for something that another possesses, or wanting to possess as much as he does.

Sloth — laziness in performance of spiritual duties. Willful stagnation in spiritual growth.

ADHERENCE TO THE GENERAL COUNSELS OF CHRIST

The Gospels of Matthew, Mark, Luke and John. The Epistles of the New Testament.

GOOD HABITS NECESSARY TO HARBOR LOVE

Humility — gentleness, meekness, obedience to God

Selflessness — concern for another's welfare

Detachment — impartiality to material goods, indifference to bodily cravings

These precepts contain God's greatest commands, and when we conform our actions to them we accept His most holy will, and display our trust in Him. **With His divine assistance we prepare ourselves for the goal of our journey: eternal life in the perfect love, peace and happiness of God.**

RESOLUTIONS

We are all invited to share in God's life
with the peace and happiness
of His supernatural love,
now on this earth and forever in heaven.

Let us respect this great offer with care
by resolving to grow in the love of God.

Let us *discover the truth* about God by
knowing the goodness of the Father.

Let us *desire the peace* of God by
loving the gifts of the Son.

Let us *develop the happiness* of God by
serving the advice of the Spirit.

AND

**Let us enjoy eternal life with God
by sharing His love with each other.**

ACKNOWLEDGEMENTS

The inspiration of this work comes from an unquenchable thirst for the salvation of souls. This thirst begins in Jesus Christ and is transmitted through the Holy Spirit. The thirst becomes a burning desire to ignite all people with the fire of God's love. For my sister Suzie and all others who ignited me by their prayers, I am eternally grateful.

Special recognition is due my father, Henry Zeiter. He provided the pain-staking effort of several edits of this book. I also thank my mother, Carol, for her insightful suggestions. Thank you mom and dad for your encouragement and contributions which fostered the completion and publication of this book.

Thanks to the many people who supported me in this work through their time and effort. Editing and encouragement were provided by Betsy Schooff, Daniel Daou, and Patrick Madrid.

I am especially grateful to my wife, Alicia. Her unceasing warmth and smiles continually encourage me. And in her supreme dignity, she emanates respect for all people which instills confidence in me and all those who are blessed with the gift of her friendship.